CW00567005

How to be Outstanding Early Years Practitioner

OTHER TITLES FROM BLOOMSBURY EDUCATION

100 Ideas for Early Years Practitioners: Supporting EAL Learners
by Marianne Sargent

100 Ideas for Early Years Practitioners: School Readiness
by Clare Ford

100 Ideas for Early Years Practitioners: Outdoor Learning
by Julie Mountain

Best Practice in the Early Years
by Alistair Bryce-Clegg

How to be an Outstanding Early Years Practitioner

Louise Burnham

BLOOMSBURY

LONDON · OXFORD · NEW YORK · NEW DELHI · SYDNEY

Bloomsbury Education
An imprint of Bloomsbury Publishing Plc

50 Bedford Square
London
WC1B 3DP
UK

1385 Broadway
New York
NY 10018
USA

www.bloomsbury.com

Bloomsbury is a registered trade mark of Bloomsbury Publishing Plc

First published 2016

British Library Cataloguing-in-Publication Data
A catalogue record for this book is available from the British Library.

ISBN:
PB: 9781472934406
ePub: 9781472934437
ePDF: 9781472934413

Library of Congress Cataloging-in-Publication Data
A catalog record for this book is available from the Library of Congress.

10 9 8 7 6 5 4 3 2 1

Typeset by Newgen Knowledge Works (P) Ltd., Chennai, India
Printed by CPI Group (UK) Ltd, Croydon, CR0 4YY

This book is produced using paper that is made from wood grown
in managed, sustainable forests. It is natural, renewable and recyclable.
The logging and manufacturing processes conform to the environmental
regulations of the country of origin.

To view more of our titles please visit www.bloomsbury.com

Contents

For an outstanding early years practitioner,

Mrs Den Hill, with love and thanks.

Acknowledgements

Thank you to all who have helped me in the writing of this book, particularly Penny Tassoni, Emma Tibbitts, Selina Moss and Den Hill for their contributions and advice. Also thanks to the Facebook group, Teaching Assistants' Support Group UK, in particular Jenny Sladden and Melanie Haxby-Smith, for answering my questions and providing such great quotes!

Introduction

What does 'outstanding' mean, and who decides whether another professional is an outstanding practitioner? If you are reading this book, it is because you would like to improve and develop what you do and what you know, so that you can become an outstanding early years practitioner in your school. It is designed to support you if you are new to the profession or to your role, or if you need support in identifying and working on key areas which will make you excel further.

You may be a newly-qualified or relatively inexperienced teacher who has found yourself working in a Reception class, or a teaching assistant who has recently moved to early years having worked further up the school; alternatively, you may also be working as an early years practitioner in a school-based nursery, but be more familiar with independent nurseries. Whatever your role, it is likely that you have bought this book as you find working with this age different from what you are used to, or would like to refresh your knowledge.

So how can this book help you? It is designed to be easily accessible and to look at the key areas which you will need to focus on when working with this age group. You will find lists and bullet points, as well as practical ideas to help you when planning and working with children. You can choose whether to read it through or dip into it if there is a particular area in which you have an interest or need more information.

You will find a range of ideas and strategies which will help you to:

- find your way around the Early Years Foundation Stage (EYFS)
- find tips for organising the classroom
- involve parents

- develop different areas of the learning environment
- look at your own continuing professional development (CPD).

As well as these areas, the book will look at planning, observation and assessment and examine the way in which you work with and relate to other professionals both within and outside your school. You will need to be able to work alongside others to plan and deliver lessons, as well as support them in writing assessments and keeping children's records of achievement up to date. Everyone who works in early years should have a clear idea about the requirements of the EYFS and understand that it is distinct from the National Curriculum.

You may also find that you need inspiration and new ideas to support you when finding yourself in different scenarios: colleagues or even training courses will be a great support, but this book will also help you in looking at ways in which you can develop outstanding practice, and will encourage you to think regularly about key areas throughout your work in the EYFS. Your role will be constantly evolving for different reasons, and you will need to be able to adapt and change with it.

As an early years professional you should be continually keeping yourself up to date with current practice through reading newspapers and early years journals. Tips for the kinds of things you should be reading will be included, along with websites and ideas which you may find useful, at the end of the book.

Chapter 1
The role of the adult in the early years

What is the role of the adult in the early years, and how do we take the first steps towards being an outstanding practitioner? As well as a passion for your job and an enthusiasm for working with children, the first step in looking at what makes you an outstanding practitioner is to think about your role. Being outstanding means that you will need to be clear on exactly what you are expected to *do*, and what you need to *know,* and how you should go about doing it. You will need to be clear both on the expectations of the Early Years Foundation Stage (EYFS) and also on the requirements of your job description, and we will be looking at both of these in this chapter.

The EYFS and what it means for the role of the adult

As you should already know, the first place you need to look is the *Statutory Framework for the Early Years Foundation Stage 2014* (see Further reading and resources, at the end of the book) which outlines what all providers must do. You will need to print it off and keep it accessible so that you can refer to it regularly. It gives a breakdown of all of the requirements of the EYFS, starting with the learning and development requirements, and 'sets the standards that all early years providers should meet to ensure that children learn and develop well and are kept healthy and safe'. You should read through and be very familiar with all aspects of this document if you are working with this age group. The EYFS focuses on the whole child and has four overarching principles which you always need to keep at the forefront of your work with young children:

1   Every child is a **unique child**, who is constantly learning and can be resilient, capable, confident and self-assured.

2   Children learn to be strong and independent through **positive relationships**.

3   Children learn and develop well in **enabling environments**, in which their experiences respond to their individual needs and there is a strong partnership between practitioners and parents and/or carers; and

4   Children **develop and learn in different ways and at different rates**.

It is not practical to look at every aspect of the document here, but a useful exercise when considering the role of the adult is to read through it from time to time and consider it in light of what you do. The introduction gives a good overview of the requirements of the EYFS and highlights the importance of each child's right to a secure, safe and happy childhood. Following the introduction, the three sections of the *EYFS Statutory Framework* are:

- the learning and development requirements (the curriculum and early learning goals for the end of the Reception year)
- assessment (the arrangements for measuring progress)
- the safeguarding and welfare requirements (this covers keeping children safe and well).

Your role, whatever your job description, will encompass all of these, and we will be looking at the different sections more closely at different stages of the book.

In practice

Have a close look at your job description. What does it tell you about your own role when working with children?

Another document which will prove very helpful to you when working with EYFS children is *Development Matters in the Early Years Foundation Stage*.

This breaks down the curriculum into age groups and has columns suggesting what adults can do and provide for children at each stage. For example under 'Communication and Language in the Listening and Attention' section for this age group, some suggestions include:

- Play games which include listening for a signal, such as Simon Says.

- Use opportunities to stop and listen carefully for environmental sounds, and talk about what sounds you can hear.

- Explain why it is important to pay attention when others are speaking.

- Choose stories with repeated refrains, dances and action songs involving looking and pointing, and songs that require replies and turn taking.

- Plan regular short periods when individuals listen to others.

You can use this document in many ways, but it is so useful when planning and assessing. It is also helpful to support adults in their roles within the classroom when working alongside children, so always keep a copy close at hand. This is an example for this aspect of the educational programme, but there are many others, and you will be covering many of them anyway as part of your daily practice. However, if you are setting out in the role, it is reassuring and helpful to dip into from time to time.

In practice

If you haven't already used it, have a look through the *Development Matters* document so that you can see examples in each of the seven curriculum areas. How might this help you in your own planning?

Roles and responsibilities of adults working in early years settings

Adults working with early years children in schools will all have different roles and responsibilities, and you should know and understand how you fit in, both within the early years team and the school as a whole. You should have a job description outlining your key responsibilities, as well as a person specification listing the kinds of qualities which you will need to have in your role. You also need to be clear about how what you are doing relates to what others in your setting are doing, as all roles are important and you will all need to work closely together as a team. Look at the job structure within your setting; if it is not clear to you, so that you can see how your role and the roles of others fit together, ask your line manager to clarify the situation for you. An ideal time for checking in, especially if there have been some changes in staffing in the school or nursery, is during your annual appraisal. (See Chapter 10 for more on this.)

The main early years job roles which are in schools and school-based nurseries include those outlined below. If your exact job title is not listed here, this may be because your local authority, school or nursery has given it a slightly different name.

Nursery manager/Early years manager and deputy

The early years manager and their deputy, if there is one, will be ultimately responsible for ensuring that the nursery or class runs smoothly. This will include everything from hiring and managing staff to ensuring that there is enough fruit for the children on a day-to-day basis. However, the key point is that the teacher or nursery leader will be answerable to them about the children's learning; activities which are planned for will need to meet the individual needs of the children and show how next steps are incorporated. Managers will also have regular meetings with teaching staff to look at children's progress and to discuss any concerns. They will also then in turn need to feed back to head teachers and be able to show how they are monitoring children's learning.

Examples of duties and responsibilities

- To be responsible for the day-to-day running of the nursery and/or Reception classes.
- To be a member of the school's management team and to contribute to the development of policies and strategies for the development of the early years.
- To ensure that the EYFS is delivered effectively.
- To be responsible for staff management, supervision and appraisal.

- To work closely with the SENCo or inclusion manager in planning for children who may have special educational needs (SEN).
- To identify any staff training needs.
- To plan, monitor, evaluate and develop the early years department.
- To order and maintain resources and equipment.
- To work effectively with other local providers such as schools and health providers.

Early years SENCo (Special educational needs co-ordinator)

In a school setting, this individual may be the SENCo or inclusion manager for the rest of the school as well, but in a larger school with a nursery attached you may also have an early years SENCo. This person is responsible for the identification, intervention and monitoring of children who have or who may have special educational needs or disabilities. Children who come into schools and nurseries may already have been recognised as needing additional support, particularly if these needs are physical or medical. However, there may be some whose additional needs have not yet been identified, for example those with learning difficulties or those who have social and emotional needs.

Examples of duties and responsibilities

- Ensuring the inclusion of every child through the identification, provision and monitoring of children who have special educational needs or disabilities.
- Working with outside professionals to ensure provision.
- Arranging meetings with parents, staff and outside agencies.
- Completing Education, Health and Care plans (EHCs) and related paperwork.
- Working with staff to support children and to provide smooth transitions as they move through school.
- Attending courses and keeping up to date with legislation.
- Implementing and reviewing the SEN policy and ensuring all staff are aware of it.
- Developing SEN resources.

Class or nursery teacher

The class or nursery teacher will take ultimate responsibility for the planning, delivery and assessment of the children's learning. However, in a nursery there will be less whole-class teaching and more individual group work than in a Reception class, due to the differing ages of the children.

Examples of duties and responsibilities

- To work in line with the *EYFS Statutory Framework*.
- To plan and implement a variety of high-quality learning activities based on whole-class, small-group and self-initiated learning.
- To create a stimulating learning environment.
- To identify pupils who may have special educational needs, or who are not yet fluent in English, and ensure that learning is appropriately differentiated and that they are able to make progress.
- To make effective use of assessment when planning and teaching.
- To use a range of resources effectively to support teaching and learning.

Teaching/Early years/Nursery assistant

As an assistant you will be asked to perform a wide range of tasks. These may relate to preparing the environment (particularly when the children are starting in the school or nursery), setting up learning activities, supporting children with tasks and contributing to record keeping. In almost all cases the job description of an early years worker will end with 'Any other duties appropriate at the line manager's discretion.' This is because it is almost impossible to list every potential duty!

Examples of duties and responsibilities

- Deliver a range of activities to children both individually and in groups.
- Use assessment and evaluation of learning to support.
- Be responsible for the organisation of the learning environment, both indoor and outdoor.
- Help with preparing and clearing up the learning environment.
- Know and work to school policies and procedures.

- Actively develop positive relationships with children and parents.
- Promote inclusion of all children.
- Act as a positive role-model.

Learning support assistant/Individual support assistant working with an individual child

You may have different job titles, but in this role you will be working with a named child who has special educational needs or disabilities. In this situation you will need support from your school's SENCo or early years manager, and also from outside agencies so that you can plan for and work effectively with the child. In addition to your own responsibilities, many will also be similar to those of the nursery assistant, above. This is because when you are working with an individual child, you will still need to be aware of what others are doing in the setting and will also work with other children. You should also be aware that this is one of the only job roles where you are actively encouraging a child to manage without you.

If you work with an individual child, you should be particularly aware of rules around confidentiality. This is because you will have access to often very personal information about the child. It is important that you do not discuss or share this with others.

Examples of duties and responsibilities

- To develop an understanding of the specific needs of the child.
- To work with the SENCo and class teacher to develop a programme of support.
- To help find and adapt materials for teaching and learning.
- The aid the child's learning as effectively as possible within a group, the class and individually, and enable them to access the curriculum and develop independence.
- To contribute to annual review meetings for the child.

Key person

This is not a specific job title but the role applies to all who work in early years settings. Their job role may be as a class teacher, early years teacher, teaching assistant, or early years assistant. The EYFS states that every child must be allocated a key person who will get to know them and their parents and to make sure that every aspect of the child's needs is met. The key worker is responsible for ensuring that 'every child's learning and care is tailored to meet their individual needs'. (*EYFS Statutory Framework 2014*).

The role also focuses on the emotional needs of the child and on getting to know them and their parents, and providing support: 'the key person must seek to engage and support parents and/or carers in guiding their child's development at home'. It also encourages parents to speak to one person rather than to different members of staff to avoid important information being lost. This ensures that the setting is kept up to date on a daily basis with what is happening and ensures that information is passed on. Nurseries and schools may do this in different ways, but one of the most popular is through having a quick meeting at the end of the day, or if this is not possible, through a day book kept in a central secure location which all staff will check daily.

The key person is also responsible for keeping records of assessment on their children and making sure that information is updated regularly. The role of the key worker is also very important for parents, as it provides consistent contact with one person and enables them to develop trust with the setting, particularly if they are vulnerable or feeling isolated themselves. This can only work to the benefit of the children and the setting, as it encourages a flow of information between parents and early years professionals. (See Chapter 2 for more on the role of the key person when working with parents.)

In addition, there will be others who come in and work in the school or nursery. These may be volunteers or students on early years courses, and they should be given an induction to policies and procedures so that they are clear about their role and what is expected of them in the setting.

Person specification

As well as being clear about your own role through your job description, all adults working in early years will also need to have certain qualities and knowledge to enable them to carry out their role effectively. Although your role and what is expected of you will be different to that of others, many of the qualities and the knowledge needed by those who work in early years will be similar. These are very important and you need to be aware of them. If the skills needed do not come easily, bear in mind that working with children may not be for you.

Crucially, you will need to have good interpersonal skills and be a good communicator, as one of the most important aspects of your role will be to encourage the development of children's language and communication skills. Communicating effectively with others in the team will also be key, and we will look at this more closely in Chapter 2. You should have a lot of patience and a good sense of humour, as very young children have short attention spans. Working with young children is extremely rewarding, but also very tiring! Be prepared.

The personal qualities and knowledge required are usually outlined in the person specification, which you will find attached to job advertisements and which will include points such as:

- full qualifications for the job role advertised

- up-to-date safeguarding training

- knowledge/experience of the EYFS

- knowledge of child development

- knowledge of health and safety issues in an early years setting

- current paediatric first-aid certificate

- ability to communicate effectively and work as part of a team

- willingness to attend staff meetings or school activities outside school hours

- willingness to undertake further training and development

- good written and oral skills

- ability to use own initiative

- creativity and flexibility

- patience and a sense of humour.

Does this sound like you? If you are currently working in an early years setting, you should be able to recognise most of the points on the list. Although this is not a full list and will vary from setting to setting, you should be aware of the basic knowledge and skills which you will need to have.

This chapter outlined the role of the adult in an early years classroom. Before we start to think about outstanding learning activities, we need to look at how we can work effectively with other people.

Chapter 2
Working with parents

The introduction of the *EYFS Statutory Framework* states that it seeks to provide 'partnership working between practitioners and with parents and/or carers'. If we look again at the four overarching principles of the EYFS, each of them underlines that:

- every child is a unique child
- children learn to be strong and independent through positive relationships
- children learn and develop well in enabling environments, in which their experiences respond to their individual needs and there is a strong partnership between practitioners and parents and/or carers
- children learn in different ways and at different rates.

As an early years practitioner, part of your role is to ensure that partnerships with parents are an ongoing part of your work with children. You should remember that parents are trusting you, in their absence, to look after their child and to act *in loco parentis*, that is, in their place. In this chapter we will look at ways in which early years professionals can communicate and develop partnerships with parents, and we will also discuss the importance of sharing information about children and supporting them in different areas. You will need to show how you work with parents as part of your day-to-day practice, particularly for those children for whom you are their key person (see Chapter 1 for a description of this role) This can only be beneficial to children, parents and everyone who works with the child because it provides:

- effective communication between home and school
- mutual support for the child's early development

- consistency of ideas
- positive reinforcement for achievements and consistency when managing behaviour
- support for assessment.

Each of these is important – to the child, the parent and the setting. We will now look at them individually and explore how they can be achieved.

Effective communication between home and school

Effective communication is a key aspect of your partnership with parents. Along with your setting, you should ensure that as many channels of communication as possible are open and available, so that parents feel that both you and the setting are approachable, and that they can speak to you if they need to (see page 22).

In practice

Consider how staff in your setting communicate with parents. Make a list of points, and think about whether you are as open and approachable as you could be.

Mutual support for the child's early development

You will be supporting the child by showing them that all adults, both at home and in the setting, are committed to supporting their learning and are taking an active interest in what they are doing each day.

In practice

Think about how you take an active interest in what children are doing. Do you communicate this to parents?

Consistency of ideas

This is helpful because the child is able to see that adults have the same thoughts about how things should be done and how their learning should be approached. The school or nursery should make sure that they are transparent in what they do and in how different areas are taught or managed. This is also evident through looking at school or nursery policies (see next page).

In practice

Consider different areas in which consistency is important. Why is this the case, and what would you do if you noticed inconsistencies between staff?

Positive reinforcement for achievements and consistency when managing behaviour

Children need to know that parents and staff communicate with each other, both when their behaviour is positive and when it is negative. In this way, there can be reinforcement when needed and positive praise for those things which are done well, and poor behaviour can be addressed. Settings should have a behaviour policy which will outline strategies and sanctions, which should be used by staff and available for parents to see. Strategies may include stickers, charts, verbal praise, or showing other staff and children, as well as parents, when behaviour is good.

In practice

Think about different ways that parents and early years workers can let children know that they are communicating with one another about what happens at home and in your setting.

Parents should also be made aware that the setting has a range of policies which cover the way in which different areas are managed, for example early years, health and safety, school visits, or equality, and that there are lots of them! Policies should be available for parents to see at any time – for example, some settings will make them available on websites, while others may have a range on display in a folder in an entrance hall. In this way, parents will know that they exist and that the school or nursery will always act in line with them. It is always better to point this out when children start school, rather than wait until a situation has occurred, for example if the parents' views are not in line with those of the school in respect to managing behaviour.

In practice

Is your behaviour policy available to parents so that they are aware of strategies and sanctions which are used to manage behaviour? Do they know about ways in which achievements are celebrated?

Support for assessment

In addition to this, an important aspect of the EYFS is that parents are encouraged to provide information about children's achievements at home. The EYFS encompasses all aspects of children's learning, from communication and language to physical development. It is important that parents are aware of this and are able to contribute to the assessment process in their own way. Many settings do this by asking parents to contribute verbally, or through writing down what the child has done, so that it can go in the child's record of achievement. Examples of this might be learning to ride a bike, counting out ingredients when making a cake or learning a nursery rhyme. The setting might provide a pro-forma which can be filled in by parents, shown to peers and then displayed, so that positive achievements are recognised. Settings may call this different things, such as a 'Wow Wall', or a 'Proud Cloud'.

The role of the key person when working with parents

'Each child must be assigned a key person. Their role is to help ensure that every child's care is tailored to meet their individual needs. . .to help the child become familiar with the setting, offer a settled relationship for the child and build a relationship with their parents.

'Providers must inform parents of the name of the key person, and explain their role, when a child starts attending a setting. The key person must help ensure that every child's learning and care is tailored to meet their individual needs. The key person must seek to engage and support parents and/or carers in guiding their child's development at home. They should also help families engage with more specialist support if appropriate.'

Statutory Framework for the Early Years Foundation Stage 2014

As can be seen from the above quotes from the *EYFS Statutory Framework*, the role of the key person and what they will need to do is significant. The role is based on John Bowlby's theory of the importance of children having strong and secure attachments in their early years, so that they feel safe and secure and have a positive sense of well-being. Up until now this has been the role of their parents or carers, with some secondary attachments to other adults, such as grandparents or close family friends. Feeling safe and secure in turn means that children develop confidence and are more likely to try new activities and experiences. It is important that children form a trusting relationship with another adult who gets to know them when they start in the setting, so that they are able to settle in with the least amount of anxiety. In order for this to happen more smoothly, the key person will also need to have a positive and trusting relationship with the child's parents and carers.

Who does the key person system benefit?

- The child: 'I know who to go to if I need help or if I am feeling sad.'
- The parent: 'I am happier to leave my child knowing that they are being individually cared for.'
- The key person: 'I am able to get to know children and their parents more deeply.'

There are several areas in which the key person plays an important role in the child's early school or nursery experience, and will need to work closely with parents.

Settling in

Many settings carry out home visits by the manager or key person for each child before they start, so that they can meet them away from the setting and have a brief informal discussion with parents and/or carers. This is beneficial for both parent and child, as they can meet and identify their key person and find out what the role means. It also means that they can talk about any concerns that parents may have, and helps both sides know who to look for when they arrive on their first day. Children and parents may also have a brief visit to the school or nursery together before the children start – in some cases there are special events, such as a welcome tea party, a few weeks beforehand – so that both parents and children can experience the setting on a normal day when other children are present, and everyone knows what to expect.

When very young children first start in a school or nursery, the environment will be different, even if they have been to a nursery or other pre-school setting before. Although some children will be more confident and outgoing than others, all are welcome and will need to be encouraged to join in. To some extent this may also include parents, as while some may have older children and will have been through the process, others may be anxious or nervous about it. At the earliest stages, staff will need to be on hand to look out for adults and children who need additional help with the settling-in process, and make a point of speaking to them each day. Through the key person process, you will be able to look out for and support those children and parents who are your responsibility (although if you are aware of other parents or children who need adult support, you should not ignore them). As a key person this period of settling in is a good opportunity to check on these children. It is likely to be staggered, which means that children will start to come in gradually, for a few hours at a time, and then build up. You will therefore have some time to speak to parents and start to get to know them. In some cases the settling-in process will need to be tailored to meet the needs of the child, for example over a more extended period if they have difficulty forming secondary attachments.

Tips for settling in – key person

- Make sure you meet parents and children before the first day, and explain the role of the key person. Devise a key person leaflet to leave with them.

- Encourage visits to the setting before the child starts.

- Find out about little things that make a difference (the child's interests, pets and so on). Will bringing in a special object help them settle in?

- Make a point of saying to parents that if they have any concerns, they should find you.

- Display photos of key people in the setting.

- Find out whether the child has had other experiences of being separated from their parents and, if so, whether particular strategies have been helpful.

- Make sure the child knows that you are their key person.

Supporting and guiding children's learning and development

Another important part of the role of the key person is that they must 'help ensure that every child's learning and care is tailored to meet their individual needs. The key person must seek to engage and support parents and/or carers in guiding their child's development at home.' How can they do this?

For those children for whom you are a key person, you will need to ensure that their care and support while in the setting is tailored to meet their individual needs. This means observing them closely and getting to know them as soon as you can, keeping closely in touch with parents and speaking with them where necessary, so that you can share information and guide children's learning at home. You can take their learning and development requirements into consideration in all aspects of what they are doing, as this covers all areas, and of course many are interrelated. A few examples are listed here:

Communication and language – You may notice that a child needs support when listening, or has problems understanding what others are saying. You will need to speak to other staff, as well as parents, and discuss how you are going to monitor this and what support may be put in place.

Physical development – You may notice that a child is awkward when holding a pencil or applying pressure when mark making, and needs support to develop these skills. This may initially mean carrying out specific activities to develop muscle strength, such as construction or play dough, but you may also need to suggest activities that parents can try at home.

Personal, social and emotional – A child who is anxious may be reluctant to join in with activities and need some encouragement, whereas a child who is confident about what they like may need support in trying different activities. As their key person, you will be able to encourage them to explore different areas and speak to parents about steps to help develop their confidence.

These are just a few examples relating to the three prime areas (see Chapter 5) of learning and development; however, there are many other scenarios that may occur and, through talking to parents, as well as colleagues, you will be able to work out steps you can take to support the child most effectively. Remember, if you have serious concerns about any aspect of a child's learning and development, you should speak to your setting's SENCo or inclusion manager.

Helping to engage with more specialist support – If, following close monitoring, the child needs to have specialist support for any reason, the key person will need to liaise with the SENCo, as well as parents and colleagues, in order to monitor the child's development. They will attend meetings alongside parents and act in a support role. For a list of the kinds of specialists you may need to engage with, see Chapter 3.

Tips for supporting and guiding children's learning and development – key person

- Make sure daily routines are consistent.
- Make sure you engage with your key children each day.
- Record and report any areas of concern.
- Speak to parents as regularly as you can.

Supporting the child's emotional well-being – This is another aspect of the key person's role. It is important that you communicate with parents and carers regularly, so that you are in touch with anything happening at home which may affect the child's learning and development, such as:

- the birth of a new baby
- a change in carer
- a parental separation or the introduction of a new step-parent
- moving house
- a serious illness or death in the family
- violence or abuse in the home.

Through close contact with parents and carers, the key person will be able to prepare for some of these transitions and work with others to find ways of supporting the child. It may be that in some cases parents are reluctant to share information about issues that are more sensitive, or they may feel that in some cases they are not relevant. As you know the child, you should always look out for any changes in behaviour, such as mood swings or tearfulness.

Children for whom English is an additional language – The EYFS states that if children's home language is not English, practitioners must ensure that they provide opportunities for them to use their home language in play and learning, while supporting the development of language at home. This is important as it shows that their home language is seen, heard and valued. If you are a key person for a child who speaks English as an additional language, you will need to show that you are monitoring their grasp of their home language through conversation with parents, as well as assessing their standard of English while they are in your care. In some cases, the key person may also speak the child's home language, and this will help them to communicate with the family – although, clearly, this is not always possible. Translators may also be available where this is needed.

Making the setting welcoming to parents

A key part of developing relationships with parents is encouraging communication and involvement. All settings, quite rightly, have security procedures in place for entering the premises, but this should not make parents feel less welcome, or stop them from visiting the school when necessary. In order to do this, parents will need to feel comfortable when bringing their child to school or nursery. You will need to remember that although some parents will have older children in school and will be familiar with the setting, for many of them coming into your class will be the first time that they have had any contact with a school environment for some time. This means that you will need to start the whole entry process by making all parents and children feel that you are approachable, and that the education of their child should be a shared experience. For some parents this may be a very different experience from their own, and you may need to encourage them to come into school in different ways. This can be through some of the following:

Welcome packs – Provide a welcome pack to parents with a list of useful information, which may make settling in easier. This may include information on timings, procedures for bringing and collecting children, breaks and mealtimes. It may also ask parents and carers to support their child's developing independence by encouraging them to practise doing up coats or fleeces, or putting on and taking off their own shoes, as well as using cutlery at mealtimes.

Open door policy – Parents should feel that they can come into the school or nursery if they need to. Although security is obviously important, parents should not feel that it is difficult for them to come in and speak to staff if they have any queries or concerns. There should be signage outside to show people how to get in, as well as notices stating the school's policy for speaking to staff at the beginning and end of the day.

Friendly entrance area – Always make parents feel welcome by ensuring that the entrance area is set up in a friendly way. This may mean having 'Welcome' displayed in different languages, showing pictures of staff with names and responsibilities and ensuring that the setting is accessible to all. Staff should also be on hand to welcome parents when they enter and also when they leave the setting, so that they can speak to them if necessary.

Tips for making parents feel welcome

- Make sure you address them correctly and call them by their preferred name. If you are unsure about what they would like to be called, ask them.
- Always smile and greet parents whenever you meet them.
- Offer to help whenever you can.
- Ensure that you mention children's achievements whenever you can.
- Remember individual facts about them, for example by asking, 'Were you able to register for the English class?'

Noticeboards and areas for parents to share information – It is useful if parents can have an area in the entrance hall that is dedicated to recent newsletters or information about the nursery or class, as well as up-to-date information about the EYFS. Leaflets can also be displayed here, for example about immunisations or starting school, or support for speakers of other languages. In some settings, information between parents and the school is also shared here, for example about children's achievements at home. For more on sharing information with parents see previous sections in this chapter.

Encouraging volunteers – Many schools encourage parents to come in to support children's learning, but this will depend on your setting's policy. Some find that it is a useful way of developing relationships with parents and would like as much help as is available. Parents can help in many ways, ranging from hearing children read to questioning them and encouraging their communication skills as they carry out activities in the nursery. Other activities such as cooking or sewing may also be possible where there are the facilities to do this, or parents may have an area of expertise which is unusual or exciting.

Tips – activities for parent helpers

- Looking at and/or reading books with children.
- Coming in to set up and work with children on an area of expertise that they may have.
- Basic everyday tasks such as sharpening pencils, or supporting children to do this.
- Helping to prepare for activities.
- Supervising children who are working on a 'structured' activity.
- Depending on their experience and confidence, observing children or noting down things that they say to support assessment.
- Simply talking to children about what they are doing, questioning them and supporting their communication skills.

Encouraging communication between home and school/nursery

There are also other ways in which schools and nurseries can encourage communication between themselves and parents:

Open afternoons or evenings – These may happen once or twice each year so that parents can come into the school or nursery to look at and discuss children's work and displays. At these events children are often encouraged to come with their parents and talk about what they have been doing in class. Any event like this will support involvement of parents in the life of the school, as well as help to develop the communication skills of the child.

School events – These may be events organised by the school or parents' association, for example a Christmas or summer fair, or a school play. These more informal events are ideal for developing relationships between parents and the setting, as they encourage communication between staff and families and support the community.

School website info – Schools and nurseries will need to ensure that websites are up to date with important information, both for existing parents and those who are interested in sending their child to the school. Usually there is a designated member of staff responsible for keeping this updated, as it is easy for it to become out of date.

Pre-school information – This is an Ofsted requirement, as all settings need to have information about children before they start. This includes names and addresses of all children, as well as contact details for both parents at home and at work, and any child-minders or other adults who will be bringing the child to school. Health needs of children also need to be documented; for example, details about any allergies or medication that the child needs to be given.

Staff email – It is helpful if staff email addresses can be given to parents, particularly to a child's key person. This is because some parents may not come into the setting regularly, for example if they work and have a child-minder, or if there is not much time to speak at drop-off or collection times. Through email they will feel that they can approach staff outside school hours if they need to, or if there is something confidential they need to discuss. All staff should have a work-based email address.

Parentmail and newsletters – Most settings now use online parentmail to provide up-to-date information on what is happening, in preference to sending out paper-based newsletters. This reduces the chance of information being lost and also ensures that all parents and carers are kept up to date regularly with what is happening.

Texts – Some settings have text contact with parents so that they can provide instant information to everyone regarding important developments, which needs to be delivered straight away – for example if children are delayed returning from a trip, or if the school is closed due to snow.

How to encourage parents to support different areas of the EYFS

Although they are all inter-connected, it is important that parents are aware of the different areas of learning and development and how they are broken down, along with the early learning goals, so that they are able to support their child's learning as much as possible. The setting can provide information about the EYFS and areas of learning through noticeboards, parentmail and pre-school information, but there should also be regular opportunities and suggestions for ways in which parents can support and encourage their child at home. Some settings run reading or maths evenings for parents and produce information packs so that parents feel more confident in supporting their child in different areas. There are a few very basic examples here, but it is impossible to list them all in the space available. You will need to constantly look out for new ideas for different ways of supporting the seven areas of learning and development; there will be more on this in Chapter 5.

You should regularly update information boards, so that these do not become 'tired' and people stop looking at them. In some settings, staff change noticeboard information and suggested activities about different areas of learning on a regular basis.

Prime areas – For the prime areas, many of these activities are common sense, and parents will instinctively do them anyway, although it is helpful to think about them from time to time in order to draw attention to how important they are.

Communication and language – This involves listening and attention, speaking and understanding. Parents are likely to be aware that most activities that they do with children involve all of these, but it is important that they give the child their full attention, as well as eye contact and being at their level when speaking to them. Talking to children and spending time with them, as well as sharing books and listening for patterns within language, enables children to develop confidence, as they are able to join in and anticipate different outcomes.

Physical development – This involves moving and handling, as well as staying healthy. In order to develop children's co-ordination and control, parents can encourage them to exercise and talk to them about the importance of a healthy diet.

Personal, social and emotional development – To support children's personal, social and emotional development it is important that parents encourage them to socialise with others and develop their confidence when trying new activities. This comes through exposing them to a variety of social situations and experiences. They will also need to support children's understanding of being able to manage their behaviour through talking about their feelings, and the consequences of poor behaviour.

Specific areas

The specific areas are more 'subject' related, but at this age parents will need to ensure that they talk to their children about the world around them and give them opportunities to widen their experience.

Literacy

Reading – Parents should be encouraged to support children as they develop their enjoyment of books and reading. This can be done in different ways, although simply taking time to sit and look at a book each day will be very beneficial to their child. Often the nursery will take part in events such as book weeks or days, or they may liaise with local libraries to provide support and encouragement to parents when children are learning to read. Some settings will give a reading talk to discuss ways of helping children and tell parents how reading is taught in the setting, and books are likely to be sent home with some form of contact between home and the setting.

Writing – Parents can support the development of children's writing skills in many ways. It is important for them to know that the physical process depends on the development of strength in the shoulder and upper arm, as well as through hand manipulation and fine motor skills. Doing activities such as skipping using a rope, throwing, or playing catch will help with this, while using construction toys (such as Lego) and also play dough will develop strength in the hands. When supporting their child during their first attempts at forming words, it is very important for all adults to be positive and interested.

Mathematics

Numbers – There are many different ways in which parents can support their children with number recognition and counting. Reciting simple nursery rhymes which involve numbers, singing number songs and playing board games will reinforce children's ability to hear and use numbers in context. Counting when carrying out day-to-day activities, such as shopping or climbing stairs, or looking for numbers in the environment, also reinforce children's understanding. Parents should also know the importance of mathematical vocabulary such as 'more' or 'less', 'altogether', 'how many?', 'in between', and so on, as without an understanding of their meaning, children will find it hard to understand some mathematical concepts.

Shape, space and measures – Mathematical language is, again, important here, particularly when comparing size, length, weight, and so on. Parents can help their children by talking about the difference in size and shape of simple objects, as well as by asking them to describe the different features of basic shapes – for example, thinking about edges, sides, curves, straight lines, and so on.

Understanding the world

Much of what children know about the world is based on conversations they have with adults, as well as through their own breadth of experience. Through showing them how different people live and through comparing similarities and differences, children will start to understand that we are all different and enjoy different things. Understanding the world also encompasses technology; this is not restricted to the use of computers, but also includes the ability to operate simple devices, such as a small, hand-held vacuum cleaner, or a remote control, or a wind-up toy.

Expressive arts and design

Parents can encourage their child by making sure that there are plenty of creative or messy opportunities for them to use different materials and tools at home (for example, cardboard for junk modelling, play dough or scissors for cutting pictures out of magazines). Their imaginations can also be encouraged through music, dance and drama in different contexts.

Chapter 3
Relationships with others

An important part of your role is being able to have good working relationships with others. These will include children and parents, and management and colleagues within the setting, as well as a variety of other professionals with whom you may come into contact. It is highly likely that you will get on with people differently – with some it will be easy to click, while others may always leave you wondering what you said to upset them! Clearly you will not have any control over how others behave, but you should always feel that you have acted in a professional and supportive way through the ways in which you approach and respond to others.

This chapter will look at ways in which you can develop effective relationships with others and think about your own professional communication skills; it will also outline the roles of some of these different professionals. Further afield, you will also have professional relationships with others outside the setting through the ways in which the school has contact with those in the local community.

How to build positive relationships and why this is important

Building and maintaining good relationships is not a matter of chance. You should always think about how you come across to others and how your actions may impact on them. This is especially true in professional situations where the consequences of poor working relationships can have an impact both on your own efficiency and that of your team. Effective relationships with parents will benefit children, parents and the setting, as important information is more likely to be shared. In order to build effective relationships, you will need to think about your own communication skills with others and the way in which you treat them. Young children will also pick up on the way in which adults around them interact, and it is important that you are a good role-model for them.

Communication with others and skills needed

When communicating effectively with both adults and children, we need to have a number of different skills:

Approachability – Make sure you smile and acknowledge people every day when you see them, however you are feeling yourself. This is not always easy but encourages others to communicate with you. Nobody will want to talk to someone who is stony faced or doesn't take the time to look up when they go past. With young children in particular you should always show that you are interested and accessible, as this is reassuring for them and encourages them to talk to you.

Openness – Show that you are able to discuss any issues as they arise. This is important because otherwise people worry and dwell on what they are going to do next. It is always better to share and discuss rather than pretend that problems are not there. This is particularly true if parents have any concerns or issues to discuss; it is always better to act first and deal with them straight away, to show that you are taking control. In each case this may mean organising a meeting or taking the time to respond to an email as soon as possible, rather than putting it off.

Empathy – The term 'walk a mile in another person's shoes' is worth considering, and you should make sure that you are sympathetic to the needs of others. Everyone has their own lives and may have problems outside work that you are not aware of. (Some people say that they come to work to forget about other things!) Look at the bigger picture and try to avoid judging people or making assumptions about their lives or why they have acted in a particular way.

Respect – Ensure that you respect others and act in a way that encourages them to respect you. If you act in an unprofessional manner, or do not pull your weight in a work environment, others may resent you and feel that they are doing your work. If there is a reason for your behaviour, and you are unable to carry out your duties, you must always say so in order to avoid bad feeling. In this way, your colleagues can help you, and in turn, you can help them when needed.

Types of communication

There are two main types of communication which we use all the time: these are called 'verbal' and 'non-verbal'. We use both when interacting with children and adults.

Non-verbal communication

A great deal of our communication with others is non-verbal and can be very powerful. It is only effective, however, if the other person can understand and respond to it. You should be aware that some autistic children, for example, may not pick up on what you are communicating to them, as they are not always aware of these types of cues. And, of course, you may also work with some adults who do not respond to them. Much of the time you will use them without thinking, but you should be aware of their impact.

Smiling and using other facial expressions – These are particularly effective if you have caught a child's eye when they are doing something which is not appropriate! You can show disapproval through frowning or shaking your head lightly, or winking and nodding if they are doing something well.

Using gestures – Simply showing a thumbs up or putting your hand up to stop a child from doing something can be useful when you catch a child's eye in the classroom.

Using body language – It is easy to use body language to show others your interest in what they are saying. Use eye contact and acknowledge what people are saying by nodding appropriately. Consider, too, the way you are standing or sitting as a means of giving attention.

Verbal communication

This is our main method of interaction with others, so although this sounds obvious, you should think about *what* you say to others and *how* you say it. Tone of voice, emphasis on particular words and the type of language you use will all affect the way in which you come across. You may also need to adapt your use of language, depending on your role within the setting and the context. A meeting, for example, will demand more formal language, while speaking to a colleague in the staff room about something that has happened that morning will be more informal.

It is also important to be professional at all times when you are in school. This means not gossiping or talking about others in a way that is negative or could be seen as such. You must also remember your responsibilities surrounding confidentiality, and should not discuss personal information about children with others unless necessary; for example, as part of a meeting concerning the child with others who may need to know. As part of the school community, you should act in a supportive way to colleagues and speak to the person concerned if you have a problem or issue which you need to discuss. Remember that positive lines of communication between staff are the most effective way of maintaining good working relationships.

In practice

Have you read your school's confidentiality policy? You are likely to have signed it, so make sure you know what is in it!

Cultural and social differences

Depending on where you work and the different cultures and nationalities within the school or nursery, you may find that there are a number of cultural or social communication differences that may affect the way in which others communicate. In some cultures, for example, making eye contact is not polite when speaking to someone. Should you be in a setting with a large number of pupils from one particular culture, or who speak English as a foreign language, then it is likely that your setting has a policy in place to support you. Ensure that you familiarise yourself with the policy, as you may be able to take advice about how you should approach certain situations. If you have any concerns, you should always seek advice from a more senior member of staff.

Using all available methods of communication

Love it or hate it, technology is here to stay. You will need to be able to use the internet and email. In many settings, newsletters and parentmail (parent emails) are sent out regularly and staff are expected to check them regularly, so that they are aware of what is happening on a daily basis. Texts may also be sent for more urgent information.

It is also important to check your school or nursery email account *at least* once a day. This is the quickest way of getting information out to people, so that everyone is aware of important information. You should not assume that people will come to you personally and tell you what is happening if you are not keeping yourself up to date. Be responsible and stay informed.

Adapting communication methods

You may need to adapt the way you communicate to allow for the needs of others. If you work with a child who has a sensory impairment, or who is on the autistic spectrum for example, you may need to use alternative means of communication such as sign language, braille or PECS (Picture Exchange Communication System). You will need to learn to adapt the way you communicate so that these children can access the curriculum. Your school or early years SENCo or inclusion manager should be able to help you with this, alongside any specialist teachers.

If you have colleagues or parents who have communication needs, always make sure you give them your full attention when speaking to them. You should also check that their understanding is clear, perhaps by summarising key points after a conversation.

Tips for having effective communication skills

- Be a good role-model to children.
- Smile and be interested in others.
- Take time to listen.
- Show respect.
- Be aware of individual differences.
- Adapt communication methods when needed.

Developing relationships with children

Because of your career choice, it is likely that you will get on well with children! However, it is worth thinking about how you interact with them, and ensuring that you are giving them your full attention as much as you can. This is particularly important for several reasons:

Communication and language is a prime area of learning and development in the EYFS – It covers all of the early years curriculum, and without being able to express themselves or understand what is happening, children will be at a severe disadvantage. You will need to observe and listen to your key children closely to ensure that their language skills are developing as they should. If you have any concerns you should speak to your SENCo or inclusion manager.

Ensure that you actively listen to children – Talking to them with your back to them, or ignoring what they are saying does not show children that you are interested or develop their confidence. Take time to listen, make eye contact and respond to their needs. As an adult, children will look to you to find out how they should respond to others themselves, so you will need to model how we communicate and develop relationships with others in a positive way.

Communication and language are linked to children's social and emotional development, as well as their behaviour – By taking the time to talk and listen to children, you are reassuring them and supporting their self-esteem, as they will learn that communication and developing relationships is a positive thing. This gives them more confidence to initiate conversations with others. It is also important that children learn to express themselves as soon as they can, so they do not become frustrated. Before children learn to speak, they are more likely to become frustrated and show impulsive and inappropriate behaviour.

Spending a day with young children is both rewarding and exhausting; in a busy working day we are often bombarded with requests, and this can sometimes be difficult. However, the importance of active listening and positive responses cannot be overstated, as children need to feel that they are heard, particularly if they are distressed or upset. For more on the different areas of learning see Chapter 5.

Working with groups

When you are working with a group of children, it may be difficult for you to give them the amount of attention they need. Some will be more demanding than others, and it can be hard to balance the needs of the group with the needs of each child. You should make sure that you arrange the group so that you can reassure children who need it and manage behaviour if necessary. If behaviour is likely to be an issue, make sure you keep the group as small as possible. Groups should not be larger than four to six children to one adult, as any larger makes it too difficult for one adult to manage the needs of each child.

Tips – working with children

- Make sure you know everyone's name.

- Find out about any needs which individuals have.

- Stay close to children who may need reassurance or whose behaviour is not on task.

- Encourage all children to talk and give their ideas.

Working with colleagues

We are all part of a number of different teams within a school. You will be part of a team of teachers or teaching assistants, part of an early years or year group team, part of a team to support a named child, part of a management team, and so on. Each of these teams will have a common purpose and, within it, members will have different responsibilities. We have all heard the cheesy quotes, such as 'There is no "I" in team' or 'Together Everyone Achieves More' (TEAM). However, it is important to remember that you will need to work together, and that the needs of children and the team should always come first. Depending on the nature of the team, regular meetings may be held and various items discussed, so that members can put their views across. It is important that each member of the team is aware of their responsibilities and that important information is shared, so that everyone is aware of what is happening.

As team members will have a range of personalities and opinions, it is likely that areas of conflict will crop up from time to time. It is important that team members talk about any issues as they arise, so that these are resolved early *within* the team. Always be aware that there is usually a reason for particular behaviour, and try to support others where you can.

Team tips

- Communicate effectively and share essential information.
- Work with each other for common goals.
- Value and respect one another.
- Have clear roles and responsibilities.
- Prepare for meetings.
- Discuss and resolve any issues as they arise.

Taking time to listen to others

Working with others can be stressful and challenging, but it can also be fun and rewarding. Depending on how you get on with people, relationships will always be different, but if others ask you for your help or advice, you should make sure that you give it; emotional support is very important. This involves supporting others through things that may be happening on a day-to-day basis, and sometimes those which occur outside the setting. When you are at work it may not always be possible to help straight away due to time commitments, but make sure you remember if you have said that you would have a chat, or go back and ask a colleague if you can help them. Taking the time to remember to ask them about something which has happened to them, or going back to check that they are okay can make a huge difference.

Working with other professionals

As well as colleagues within the school, you are likely to work with other professionals. Unfortunately, due to recent large cuts in school and council budgets, there are now fewer external and advisory teachers or health professionals coming into schools and nurseries to advise staff. Although this is the case, depending on your budget and location, it is likely that you will work alongside a number of different professionals at some point, and you will need to know what they do. Many of them will support children who have special educational needs, and your SENCo or inclusion manager will organise visits where possible.

Occupational therapist (OT) – The OT will work on the development of children's fine motor skills and give them support in strengthening the muscles of the hands.

Physiotherapist – The physiotherapist will work on the development of gross motor skills and give exercises and support in strengthening large muscle groups.

Autism advisory teacher – This teacher may come in to the setting to observe and support the development of children's social and communication skills.

Educational psychologist – The educational psychologist may come in to assess children where staff have concerns about areas of their development. Parents will be involved, and it is likely that assessments will take place to enable the educational psychologist to make a diagnosis.

Speech and language therapist – Some schools have speech and language therapists on site if there is a unit; otherwise the child will usually need to go to them for a series of block therapy sessions. They will also give parents work to do with children at home, and occasionally for staff to do in school.

Sensory support teacher – This teacher will come in to advise staff on how to best support children who have a hearing or visual impairment; they may also provide equipment and regular visits to check on children's progress.

Behaviour support teacher – This teacher may come in to observe children in order to support staff and parents with behaviour issues.

All of these advisory staff are likely to meet with you if you are a teacher or teaching assistant working with the child, alongside parents, the SENCo or the inclusion manager. In this way, everyone will be able to put their ideas forward so that you will be able to devise an EHC for the child.

Developing local links and community cohesion in the early years

As part of your school or nursery, you are also part of the local community, and it is important to develop links with members of the local community. This supports children's understanding of the world and their place within their own immediate environment. Although developing community cohesion, as it is called, is the responsibility of all staff, your setting should have a policy, and this means that you will be encouraged to work with others in the community where possible. Examples of this in action in nurseries and Reception classes might include:

- supporting local libraries by visiting them or asking them to come and speak to the children to support book weeks or a summer reading challenge

- inviting professions who help others in to come in as part of a topic on 'People who help us', such as police, firemen, dentists, doctors

- working with local churches during different religious festivals, perhaps holding a service or having a concert alongside them

- working with local old people's homes and visiting the elderly, or asking them to visit the school, perhaps to hear children read

- visiting shops or supermarkets as part of topics to find out about what happens there.

All of these situations give children opportunities to develop their social skills as well as their knowledge, through speaking to people and asking their own questions, and broadening their social experience. It is also good for the school to be integrated and to be seen to be part of the local area through having wider positive relationships.

Chapter 4
Enabling environments

'Children learn and develop well in enabling environments, in which their experiences respond to their individual needs.' This overarching principle from the *Statutory Framework for the Early Years Foundation Stage 2014* shows us the importance of providing young children with surroundings and activities which are stimulating and give them opportunities to explore, as well as through positive relationships between parents and practitioners. In this chapter we will look at indoor and outdoor classrooms, and spaces which children visit on trips, as well as considering ways in which you can keep the learning environment safe.

The non-statutory guidance for the development matters aspect, which is available at www.early-education.org.uk and www.foundationyears.org. uk, gives us suggestions for the kinds of resources which might be provided in enabling environments, and is also divided into each strand under areas of learning. This can be handy for less-experienced practitioners, as well as those who are looking for new ideas, and is easy to refer to. It is also helpful as it shows how the EYFS principles run through what we do in our practice.

What should the learning environment provide?

As stated in the *EYFS Statutory Framework*, young children need to be provided with stimulating, organised and informative surroundings, with a wide range of activities available in order to enable their learning. They should see that the learning environment is organised, and learn through the examples of adults how to keep it tidy, happy and safe, so that they can develop their independence and confidence. This will not happen by accident, and you will need to make sure that you are providing a range of activities that meet the needs and interests of the children. Displays should be fresh and have a clear purpose, with a variety of interactive content. There should also be a clear representation of different subjects and cultures. As a starting point you will check that different areas of the learning environment are clearly labelled and accessible to all children.

Keep different areas of the room clearly labelled and accessible to everyone

Have a look around your setting with a child's eye. Different spaces in the room should be set aside for mathematics, literacy, creative and expressive activities, understanding the world through exploration, and so on. These should be clearly labelled and have a range of resources available to children, so that they can access them independently. Even if they are not able to read the labels, children will be starting to pick up on the fact that print in the environment provides information, and as adults we should be pointing out what the labels mean when we are supporting them during learning activities. Numbers should also be evident as much as possible around the environment, for example 'Four children can work/play here', 'Three in the listening corner' or 'Can you count the steps?' In addition, there should be general information displayed around the environment that encourages children to look at print, for example 'Welcome to the Red Room' or 'Mr Varney's classroom'. There should also be labels at the children's level of words such as 'door' or 'window' so that children get used to seeing the words.

There are many websites available from which you can print off both plain and themed labels for children (see Further reading and resources for suggestions); use these, or you can of course devise your own. However, you should be careful and make sure that you use labels which contain recognisable fonts at this stage, and consider whether you are teaching the children basic or joined-up script for letter formation. There will also be variations between scripts, for example 'a' 'f' or 'g' are sometimes formed differently. There are some fonts that are free to download if you are teaching joined-up script, which is helpful when making your own labels, so that children see the same font as is in the environmental print. Similarly, when printing off numbers, take care to ensure that the number '4' is written in the same way that you are teaching the children to write it – we should not make assumptions about what children know and are able to recognise.

You will also need to make sure that the environment is accessible to every child. If you have children in your setting who have special educational needs, for example, you should check that the learning environment is not a barrier to their learning due to the way in which it is set up. Whatever their learning needs, children should be able to access all activities. This does not necessarily just mean physically moving around; it might mean checking that they are able to see or hear when sitting on the carpet, or that they have any specialist equipment which they need to support their learning. If you are aware that they do not have all that they need, it is important that you speak to your SENCo or inclusion manager as soon as possible. You should also keep an eye out for any as-yet-undiagnosed learning needs which may make learning less accessible to them.

Role-play area – This is always a fun and creative area to organise. At the medium-term planning stage, you and your colleagues should start to think about how you will organise and label the role-play area for various topics. In some cases, you might decide to do this with groups of children so that they can practise making labels of their own. It can be time consuming to gather resources, particularly if you are working on a new topic or do not have everything you need; it is worth storing them for use the following year if you are likely to repeat the topic. However, the role-play area will be more stimulating for children if you have 'real' items. For example, if your role-play area is a garden centre, you can use flower pots and potholders, seed packets and children's gardening tools. Where you have large numbers of children who may be using the role-play area, it may be too difficult or expensive to organise lots of resources, and you might be able to ask children to bring some in for the duration of the topic.

Literacy area – This may be divided into areas for reading, such as a book or quiet corner, and areas for listening and areas for writing. The reading area should be away from other potentially noisy parts of the room, such as the role-play area, so that children can share books quietly. It is easy to make the area cosy and comfortable with posters, cushions and magazine racks; you could also lower the ceiling or include fairy lights to make it more appealing.

As well as being clearly labelled, the writing area should have a large number of resources available for children to use: pencils, chalks, crayons and other items for mark making should be easily accessible. There should also be sound or alphabet cards/charts for children to refer to and use, and blank postcards and plenty of paper (scrap or lined), whiteboards or other materials to write on.

Tips for the writing area

- Have two children in charge of keeping the area tidy and organised and change them every week or two.

- Have a pinboard available so that children can display their writing straight away.

- Decide on a member of staff to keep this area replenished: look in charity shops for pads, old diaries and other things to write on.

- Ask the school office staff to save envelopes which have been opened: children can re-use them in the writing corner and seal them with masking tape.

- Ask children to label the writing area and pencil pots: if you ask them to write different numbers on each pot, this can encourage them to develop their 1:1 counting skills – '3 in here' or '6 in here'.

Mathematics area – In the same way, the mathematics area should have a range of accessible resources and number displays so that children are able to refer to them. These are particularly important and can be neglected, as it is often the literacy displays that are easier to devise. There should also be labelled trays containing collections of items that can be sorted or placed in repeating patterns, such as peg boards or bead strings. Puzzles, playing or number cards, dominoes and dice (large and small) and other resources should also be available. Simple interactive displays to promote different aspects of the mathematics curriculum can also be very effective, for example putting out egg boxes and asking children how many ways they can put three beads into them; or collecting data using named clothes pegs clipped onto a 'Yes or No' board in order to ask a different question each week such as 'Do you walk to school?' Check with your numeracy co-ordinator to see if you use a particular scheme further up the school that you could initiate in nursery or Reception, such as Numicon.

Creative or painting area – If possible, children should be able to independently access creative activities such as cutting and sticking, painting and drawing, junk modelling and other open-ended creative tasks. There will need to be a range of materials available, again which are accessible to them at all times. It is important that adults demonstrate how to use the creative area and keep it tidy so that children know exactly what is expected.

Understanding the world and investigative area – This is an area in which you can be really creative. Builders' trays, either inside or outside, magnifying glasses, digital cameras, 'real' resources such as compost, turf or logs, seeds and other natural materials will make these kinds of activities really fun for children. If you have space, go for a permanent interactive display so that children can regularly explore natural materials which tie in with your topic.

Children will also need to be able to access different kinds of technology within the learning environment. This may be through the use of an interactive whiteboard or laptops, digital cameras, CD players or iPods/MP3 players, toy vacuum cleaners or floor robots and other programmable toys. There are many interactive programs available for whiteboards to support children's learning; even at this young age children should be able to use them responsibly.

In practice

Take a look around your classroom and do an audit of the different areas. Are they all clearly identified and clearly labelled?

General classroom displays

As well as providing different areas in the room for areas of learning, your general classroom displays will need to be kept tidy and up to date. You will need to know your school policy for displays: in some schools all work will need to be mounted and an explanation of the learning activity or an objective included; in others a simple heading is all that is needed. Children's work should always show the name of the child. If you are working in a school, the art co-ordinator should also be able to tell you how often displays will need to be changed, and whether there is a rota for corridor and around-the-school displays.

Depending on your role, you may be asked to design the display or be told what you need to do; make sure you are clear about this if you are working to someone else's guidelines. Displays may be used for many reasons:

- to show pupils' work to others
- to brighten the environment
- to provide information
- to celebrate and share children's achievements
- to celebrate diversity
- to provide a learning resource.

If the display is of children's work, if at all possible there should be examples from all of the children in the nursery or class, and these should be clearly labelled with their names so that they are able to identify them. Young children will be very excited to see their artwork or writing on the wall or displayed on a table. There should be a clear heading in the display and an explanation of the learning which took place around it, for example, 'We took pictures of our faces and made these modelling clay ones. Can you match the picture to the modelling clay face?' In some settings the area of learning and the learning objective are also displayed. Make sure that if you have displays high up on the wall, any headings or questions are visible to children; there is little point in putting up labels which they cannot see due to their height. You may also have labels or areas which identify class helpers or table monitors, such as 'Today's helping hands are. . .'; there may be a birthday wall, or a 'word of the day'. Some classes have a self-registration area as children become more independent, so that they can simply move their name or picture as they come into class. All of these things give ownership to the children and add to the environment.

As well as wall displays, there are other ways of showing children's work and enhancing the learning environment:

Hanging displays – Both horizontal and vertical hanging displays can look really good in the indoor and outdoor learning environments, especially if, for example, work is laminated to add weight and extra protection. 'Bunting' made from children's work, such as handprints, can also look very effective. However, you will need to be careful that the display does not interfere with any indoor sensors or alarms, as you will not be very popular if so!

Interactive displays – These are always very effective, although they will need checking regularly as – surprise surprise – children will interact with them, and items can become lost or broken. Make sure you don't leave out anything that is irreplaceable or precious. Children will sometimes bring items in to add to these displays; you will need to point out to them and their parents/carers that they should not bring in anything that is irreplaceable.

3D displays – These can really enhance wall displays: for example, if the children are learning about houses, they could paint onto cereal boxes which could be put up as a street, or lanterns could be strung across the board as part of a Chinese New Year display. The only issue might be that adults can knock them, so choose a board that is out of the way and ideally not in a corridor.

Window displays – Window displays can be very effective, especially if you use tissue or other opaque paper which lets some light through. However, be careful not to cover the whole window and ensure that there is sufficient light for the children to work.

Refreshing and renewing displays

It is a good idea for a member of staff to check on displays regularly to tidy them up, as young children (or adults!) may brush against them and knock off borders or parts of a 3D display. It often doesn't take long to tidy up using a staple gun. As a general rule it is not a good idea to take down a display until you have prepared a new one to take its place and have time to put it up. Blank walls always look bare, and unless you set a specific time aside, you may find that they are left empty for a while before you have time to put up the new one. If displays have been up for a long time, you should change them, as children will get into the habit of not looking at them.

Other aspects to consider when looking at the learning environment

In addition to keeping the learning environment labelled and accessible to children, you will also need to ensure that you do the following:

- Get to know children, observe and talk to them and find out about what interests them.
- Change and vary materials according to the topic or children's interests.

- Make sure resources are accessible so that children can help themselves.
- Be proactive in keeping the learning environment safe and organised, and set a good example so that children do the same.
- Keep the environment comfortable and free of distractions where possible.

Get to know children and find out what interests them

It is important that you get to know your key children in particular (see Chapter 1) so that you can plan and provide resources accordingly. In order to do this, you will need to observe them so that you can see the kinds of activities which they particularly enjoy and choose to do. Take some time (when you are not carrying out adult-led activities) to observe the kinds of things that are popular with children. Construction activities, role-play and messy play, for example, always tend to be well used and encourage open-ended activities, but you may find that you have a child in your setting who is particularly interested in the planets, or who knows all about trains. If you know that one child loves to dance, you could set aside an area of the room or outside area with a CD player.

Make sure you are aware of any special interests. Encourage children to follow their interests; provide support and resources accordingly.

Change and vary materials and resources according to the topic or children's interests

You will need to have a wide range of activities available for children to choose from in order to cater for their various interests. Clearly some resources and materials (for example the role-play area, investigative tables and displays) will change by topic so that children have a selection. It is a worthwhile activity to check through resources once in a while, to see what you have and to check that all the pieces are still intact, as over time different materials will become broken and pieces will go missing.

Make sure resources are accessible so that children can help themselves

It is important that children are aware of the layout of the learning environment and where things are kept so that they can take out and put away items as and when they are needed. When children first come into the setting they will need to be shown where things are, and should also be encouraged to help one another to find what they need.

Be proactive in keeping the learning environment safe and organised and set a good example

Always act as a good role-model to children and ensure that you are demonstrating how to keep the environment safe, tidy and organised. This may be subtle, for example picking up tissues off the floor if you see them, or obvious, such as discussing with children the importance of keeping a room tidy and clean for everybody to use. This promotes a feeling of shared ownership and collaboration while encouraging children to look out for any hazards.

In practice

Look around your learning environment with the children and think about safety. Is it tidy and are chairs pushed in? Are fire exits clear? Are bookcases and shelves stacked safely and coats off the floor? This might be a good exercise from time to time, as it will encourage everyone to keep their eyes open.

Keep the environment comfortable and free of distractions where possible

Children will not be able to learn in situations which are uncomfortable or which take their mind off what they are doing. If you can see that children are not focused, or if they tell you what is wrong, you will need to stop the activity or move away from the problem. You should always ensure that:

- the environment is kept at a suitable temperature
- there are no distractions (noise or other disturbances) from other children
- there is enough space to work on the activity comfortably
- blinds are pulled down or windows opened if needed
- if you are lucky enough to have air-conditioning, you know how to use it.

Sometimes there are external forces or distractions that you cannot control, such as someone cutting the grass, or building work being carried out close by. In this case you may sometimes need to change your plans or move children away, as there is no point in continuing if children are unable to focus. Similarly, if there is weather which distracts children, such as strong wind, heavy rain or snow, it may be worth stopping what you are doing and using it as a learning opportunity. Part of being an early years worker is having to be flexible.

Tidying up

Tidying up should be a shared activity, and children should be jointly responsible for keeping the learning environment in an acceptable state. In some settings, practitioners use 'Tidy-up music' and children know that when they hear it, it is time to put things away. Others may make a particular sound or turn the whiteboard to a 'Tidy-up picture'. Sometimes these may also be timed, so that children can see how quickly they do it, although this can sometimes cause them to get excited and rush, rather than put things away neatly and sensibly. However, these kinds of signals put the onus onto the children to take responsibility for keeping their environment tidy, and to learn when it is time to stop.

Parental help with resources

Parents can be a fantastic help with supplying resources for early years settings, but they need to know what to bring in. It can be awkward to be helpfully given lots of large items such as boxes which you may not need! If you are able to list items on your school or nursery website and keep this up to date, this is usually the most effective way of ensuring that they can find out quickly, and you can refer them to it. Obvious items such as scrap paper and junk modelling boxes as well as old toys in good condition are almost always useful if you can store them, as long as you do not have too many. Parents may also be able to provide specialist items; for example, an optician may be able to lend you old glasses and posters for your role-play area, or a hairdresser may provide old shampoo bottles or hair curlers. When developing your outdoor area, you may also be able to ask for larger resources such as drainpipes for water play, or stepping stones made from cut-up logs. You need to keep parents up to date with topics in case they are able to provide support in other areas. (For more on parental support see Chapter 2.)

School visits and trips

Children in the EYFS will need to go out of the setting and explore different aspects of the local environment, as the EYFS curriculum encourages this. Children enjoy exploring with their peers and it makes for an exciting time. However, you will need to ensure that you have carried out a risk assessment in advance by walking along the route and visiting the site. This is because you may not always be aware of the risks involved. An example of this might be a visit to a local library or shop – you may be able to walk, but there could be issues with the route, such as roadworks or other disruptions, which mean that you have to change your route or cross the road in a different place. When you arrive, you will need to know where children will put coats or eat their lunch or go to the toilet, as well as the name of the person to ask for. As a newly qualified practitioner, you will need to be accompanied by an experienced member of staff during your probationary year, so they will be a helpful guide, and you should go through your checklist with them prior to the visit.

The outdoor learning environment

Outdoor provision is an important aspect of the EYFS learning environment. It should be seen as another classroom, and you will still need to ensure that children's learning is enabled in all areas of the EYFS curriculum. The outdoor classroom should include a variety of activities which change regularly; these should not just be indoors activities replicated outdoors! Keeping it tidy and organised can take up some time, and you may need to have a rota system with other staff as well as the children so that you are not constantly tidying it. Some items cannot be left outside, and you will need to get larger items out and put them away on a daily basis. It should include a writing and creative area, and labelled storage spaces where children are able to access basic equipment. As with the indoor classroom, the outdoor learning area should be kept as organised as possible. Clearly this can present problems due to weather and general wear and tear, so it will need to be checked regularly; most settings will have a rota for this. Always check the outside area in the mornings in case any foxes or other animals have made a mess or caused damage overnight. You will need to have outside storage, for example a locked shed, so that large equipment such as bikes, trikes and scooters can be put away. In addition you will need to have a covered area with secure cupboards, so that resources can be put away safely and stay clean and dry when not in use. Children will not be able to access some items without adult support; certain items will need to be taken out and put away each day, although the children will be able to help tidy up and ensure that the outside area is kept clean. Gates and fences should also be checked regularly to ensure that they remain safe so that children cannot hurt themselves or leave the area without an adult.

Different areas will need to be clearly labelled (as with the indoor classroom) but make sure that signs and labels are laminated and changed when they become tired, and (similarly to the indoor classroom) you will also need to ensure that there are different areas for children to access resources.

If you are lucky enough to have an outdoor tap or water butt, this can be very useful for a water area, as children will be able to help themselves and develop their independence. However, you will need to observe them closely, particularly in colder weather.

For ideas on books to help you with the outdoor environment, see the Further reading and resources section.

Health and safety in the learning environment

This is a big consideration. Train yourself to look out for health and safety issues and ensure that you point things out to children, so that they learn to be responsible. Make sure that you are always vigilant and proactive, and teach children to behave in the same way. (For more on this, see Chapter 7.)

Chapter 5
Areas of learning and development

Is it necessary to include a chapter on the areas of learning and development? It seems wrong not to, in a book designed to support becoming an outstanding early years practitioner. The *EYFS Statutory Framework* states that 'the seven areas of learning and development must shape educational programmes in early years settings' and 'each area of learning and development must be implemented through planned, purposeful play and through a mix of adult-led and child-initiated activity'. This chapter is designed to help you look closely at each of the areas of learning and development and to consider exactly what is expected by the time children reach the end of Reception, and each of the early learning goals. It will look at each in turn and at what you need to do in order to implement them in an outstanding way. You can look at it alongside Chapter 6.

Characteristics of effective teaching and learning

The characteristics of effective teaching and learning are a good starting point when looking at the areas of learning and development, as they are about the way in which children learn. You will need to consider this as part of your general observations of children, so that you can think about the opportunities and support which you provide during learning activities.

Playing and exploring – This aspect of children's learning determines their willingness to 'have a go' as well as their confidence in finding out about new things. You will need to look at the way in which they approach unfamiliar activities – are they keen to try them, or do they tend to favour those which they have tried before? Some children will lack confidence and need some encouragement to move away from familiar situations. Make sure there are plenty of open-ended tasks available so that children have lots of opportunities to explore, and provide support if they are anxious about getting involved.

Active learning – This is about children's motivation and resilience, and whether they can keep going if they encounter any problems. Some children will move on to the next thing if things are not going their way, while others will stay focused until they have completed the task. You will need to look at whether they persevere with activities and enjoy their achievements. If you offer support in these situations to encourage them to continue, you must make sure you do not 'take over' with these children; resist the temptation to finish tasks for them.

Creating and thinking critically – This is the way in which children develop ideas and think of ways in which to tackle problems through developing their own strategies and ways of working in order to succeed. It is important for them to be given challenges which allow them to develop their problem-solving skills in different ways. You will need to look at whether they try to think things through for themselves or if they wait for others to initiate their ideas.

The areas of learning and development

The seven areas of learning and development are divided into 'prime areas' and 'specific areas'. The reason for these different titles is that before children are able to fully access the specific areas, they will need to be secure in the prime areas. When working with the youngest children, it is therefore important to strongly target the prime areas first, as these skills are needed in order to learn effectively. Gradually the balance of development is expected to shift towards being more equal and balanced between the seven areas, as children become ready for school and work through the Reception year. Within the prime and specific areas, learning is subdivided further; the following breakdown also includes some ideas and hints for developing each of the areas. For ease of reference, the early learning goals (ELGs) are also included under each heading so that you can see what is expected at the end of the Reception year.

Prime areas

These are the areas of communication and language, physical development, and personal, social and emotional development. Each one is further divided into different sections.

Communication and language

This area is key, as it will affect all aspects of children's learning and development. Not only is it a way of developing relationships with others and learning social skills, but it is also a means of them organising their own thoughts so that they can start to rationalise and link different experiences together. Children will learn how to communicate through listening and watching to see how others interact with one another, so it is important to show them positive examples.

Although it is difficult in a busy setting, you should use all opportunities which are available to communicate with children and give them your personal attention while doing so. Making eye contact and getting down to their level whenever possible is also important, so that they can see you are interested; this in turn makes children more likely to initiate communication with others. Children will need to feel confident and comfortable in their surroundings to want to ask questions and find out about the world around them.

Communication with children in your setting who speak English as an additional language is also important to consider, and is discussed in more detail at the end of this chapter.

Listening and attention – ELG: *'Children listen attentively in a range of situations. They listen to stories, accurately anticipating key events, and respond to what they hear with relevant comments, questions or actions. They give their attention to what others say and respond appropriately, while engaged in another activity.'*

Listening to others is something that adults sometimes forget to do. We are often caught up in our own lives and thoughts, and do not take the time to focus on what others are saying to us. If you look carefully at this early learning goal, we are asking children be able to listen attentively and respond appropriately; this is not easy for adults, let alone young children! It can be helpful to encourage children to think about listening in different situations. For example, taking them on a listening walk and asking them to just tell you what they can hear, or asking them to distinguish between different sounds as part of a game. Make sure that children know what listening means. Always check with children who don't seem to follow instructions to make sure that they can hear you, particularly if they are prone to coughs and colds, as these can prevent them from hearing properly.

Tip

Check children's hearing by asking them to listen to sounds which are out of sight or behind a screen.

Understanding – ELG: *'Children follow instructions involving several ideas or actions. They answer "how" and "why" questions about their experiences and in response to stories or events.'*

Following instructions involving several ideas takes practice. Often we give quite complicated instructions to children, for example, 'Come in, take off your coat, put your book bag in the box and sit down.' This is quite a complicated set of instructions for a very young child, particularly if, for example, the first – taking off their coat – demands quite a bit of concentration and time to complete! You may need to repeat, or go back and check that they have understood. Always speak clearly and remember when you are working with children not to make assumptions about what they have and have not understood. In addition, children may have communication difficulties of which you are unaware because they are not as yet identified, or because parents have not informed you. You should always check with parents or carers first if children do not seem to understand.

Tip

When sharing books with children, check their understanding by asking them to point things out: resist the temptation to show them everything.

Speaking – ELG: *'Children express themselves effectively, showing awareness of listeners' needs. They use past, present and future forms accurately when talking about events that have happened or are to happen in the future. They develop their own narratives and explanations by connecting ideas or events.'*

At this stage, young children's speech will still be developing and they will be taking cues from those around them. They need to practise in order to consolidate what they know, and will sometimes find it difficult to remember everything, as language is complex. In addition, children often find it difficult to think things without saying them; this is all part of their language development. They may also need to say things aloud in order to process them. However, 'showing awareness of listener's needs' is the key point here.

Children may also need to be reminded about what you have asked them, or be given support in focusing their responses. Remember to model the correct way of speaking to children, rather than correcting them and saying, 'That's wrong.' For example, if they speak to you using immature language such as 'He runned after me and I didn't like it', children are in fact applying rules of language which they have heard in other contexts. Your reply should be, 'He ran after you? Did you tell him that you didn't like it?' In this way you are demonstrating the right use of the word. Always give children time to speak and think about what they are going to say; try not to rush them to complete words or sentences, or interrupt and speak for them.

Tip

Make sure there are plenty of interesting items in the learning environment so that children and adults can talk about them.

Adapting communication – For children who have communication difficulties, you will of course need to take extra time so that they do not feel pressured. Some children may need to communicate using Makaton, sign language or other visual means, and you may need to have additional training.

Physical development

The area of physical development is again one which affects all areas of learning and development. Through using their bodies, children find out about the world and how their actions affect their surroundings – and through learning to control their muscles, they become able to run and play with others, explore their environment and develop their physical stamina. Physical development incorporates many of the skills which children need in order to learn effectively, including holding a pencil correctly for writing. They should also be developing an understanding of the importance of physical exercise and why they need to do it to keep healthy, as well as discussing the importance of keeping safe.

Moving and handling – ELG: *'Children show good control and co-ordination in large and small movements. They move confidently in a range of ways, safely negotiating space. They handle equipment and tools effectively, including pencils for writing.'*

Children naturally need to move and exercise their bodies; as they grow and develop, they will learn to use them in different ways. This will develop naturally in most cases, although children will need to be given opportunities to exercise and develop their muscles. You will need to give children opportunities to develop their skills both in large and small movements. Make sure the outside area is always accessible to children and has a good range of equipment which enables them to develop different muscle groups, for example through the use of stepping stones, climbing equipment, bikes and scooters, and hula hoops. Encourage children who find holding a pencil difficult to develop their fine motor skills in other ways, such as through threading, using tweezers, or playing with small construction toys or play dough.

Tip

Don't ask children to sit still and listen for long periods. Remember that very young children find it difficult to do this and should not be expected to – nor should they be told off when they are unable to do it.

Health and self-care – ELG: *'Children know the importance for good health of physical exercise, and a healthy diet, and talk about ways to keep healthy and safe. They manage their own basic hygiene and personal needs successfully, including dressing and going to the toilet independently.'*

Most children between the ages of three and five will be developing their independence at dressing and going to the toilet on their own. Encourage them to do as much as possible for themselves and remind them about the importance of washing their hands! You may need to show them how to do this – again, never assume that they know what it means. They should also be taught about healthy eating and about keeping themselves safe, and this should be discussed regularly.

Tip

Encourage children who need help with fastenings to ask another child, rather than always ask an adult. Encourage them to help one another. Have pictorial instructions on the toilet wall above the basins to remind them of the sequence for washing their hands.

In practice

What are the routines in your setting when children first start to stay for lunch? Do you observe what they can do independently, such as using a knife and fork? How often do you discuss healthy eating and what they have had for lunch?

Personal, social and emotional development

This prime area of children's development is directly concerned with children's confidence and the way in which they are able to manage their emotions. In order to develop in other areas, children will need to have the confidence to try new things, meet new people and understand why we need to behave in a particular way when we are with others. Children who have come from backgrounds which are secure and safe and where they are given unconditional love are likely to find some aspects of this easier.

Self-confidence and self-awareness – ELG: *'Children are confident to try new activities, and say why they like some activities more than others. They are confident to speak in a familiar group, will talk about their ideas, and will choose the resources they need for their chosen activities. They say when they do or don't need help.'*

This is about how we can support the development of children's confidence and self-esteem. Children need to be given opportunities to make their own choices and decisions so that they become more confident in their own abilities. They should be given responsibilities within the setting, for example giving out fruit or being in charge of keeping a particular area tidy. You will also need to make sure you give children your attention and praise so that they continue to be motivated by their achievements.

Tip

Make sure there are opportunities for children to show their achievements to others in order to develop their confidence and self-esteem.

Managing feelings and behaviour – ELG: *'Children talk about how they and others show feelings, talk about their own and others' behaviour, and its consequences, and know that some behaviour is unacceptable. They work as part of a group or class, and understand and follow the rules. They adjust their behaviour to different situations, and take changes of routine in their stride.'*

This can be difficult for young children and we need to discuss its importance with them regularly. They may need support to be able to manage their feelings and behaviour, and it is important to take time to listen and allow children to talk through their feelings when they tell us about what has happened. We should ensure that children are aware of rules and why we have them, and discuss this with adults. Always use language with them which separates the behaviour from them, for example, 'That was a silly thing to do!' rather than 'What a silly girl you are!' (For more on this, see Chapter 8.)

Tip

Make sure children are aware of the consequences of what they do and the fact that it is their choice to do the right thing: 'If you hurt Jamie, your name will be put on the sad face', i.e. 'You have chosen to do this, so this will happen.'

Making relationships – ELG: *'Children play co-operatively, taking turns with others. They take account of one another's ideas about how to organise their activity. They show sensitivity to others' needs and feelings, and form positive relationships with adults and other children.'*

Learning to play co-operatively with others and take their needs into consideration may be difficult for some children, while others may seem to manage very easily. As adults we may need to encourage children to mix with their peers and develop new relationships through a range of activities and games which require them to take others' needs into consideration and allow turn taking. As well as praising those who show consideration towards others, you will need to talk any issues through with them as they occur, and encourage those who play well and co-operate with one another.

Tip

Model positive relationships with others, and particularly key children in the setting, so that children can see the benefits of this.

Specific areas

These areas relate to literacy, mathematics, understanding of the world, and expressive arts and design. As well as starting to learn to read, write and explore mathematics, children will be exploring different aspects of their world.

Literacy

Reading and writing, even in its simplest form, is one of the most difficult aspects of what we expect children to be able to do by the end of the EYFS. Children will need to have access to a wide range of activities and resources to support their reading and writing skills, so that they can develop and link them together. They are closely connected to the prime area of communication and language, as children will need to have the language to decode text and to put their thoughts into words. It is likely that phonics will be approached in a particular way in your setting through the use of a specific phonics programme. Whatever your role in the setting, you will need to be trained in this and know how to use it so that you can support children effectively in the process.

Reading – ELG: *'Children read and understand simple sentences. They use phonic knowledge to decode regular words and read them aloud accurately. They also read some common regular words. They demonstrate understanding when talking with others about what they have read.'*

Reading involves putting together a series of complex actions. In order to learn to read, children will need to have a working knowledge of their sounds and be able to link and blend them together to form words, as well as a language-rich environment so that they can practise decoding letters and sounds. You can support children as they begin to learn to read through regularly sharing books with them and using environmental print to point out text and draw their attention to its use in context. You will also need to have time each day to read books with children to develop and encourage a love of reading, and support parents in doing the same through sending books home for children to share.

Reading tips

- Spend time each day looking at books with children.

- Sing plenty of songs and rhymes which encourage children to listen for patterns and rhymes in language.

- Always give the child 'ownership' of the book if they are reading it to you by letting them hold it and turn the pages themselves.

- Give children time to 'have a go' and look at initial sounds, and avoid telling them what the word is.

- Encourage the child to use all the cues available (picture, phonics, context) to help them to read the word.

In practice

How regularly are you able to read with children? Do you encourage parents and other volunteers in to the classroom to hear children read? How much support and advice do you give to them about how to do this?

Writing – ELG: *'Children use their phonic knowledge to write words in ways which match their spoken sounds. They also write some irregular common words. They write simple sentences which can be read by themselves and others. Some words are spelt correctly and others are phonetically plausible.'*

Children will start mark making from an early age, and will enjoy experimenting using a variety of media. These may include sand, shaving foam, paints, cornflour and water, and other sensory means, as well as pencils, paper and whiteboards. Learning to write is a process which will follow or happen at the same time as reading, as children start to be able to link sounds and letters and to use these to form words. They will also need to develop the motor skills and hand–eye co-ordination necessary through cutting, threading, puzzles and other activities which rely on using fine manipulative skills. As these skills develop, children will start to copy and form the letters which represent the sounds they have been learning.

> **Tip**
>
> Look out for left-handed children, and make sure they are holding pencils using the correct grip.

Mathematics

Mathematics is a wide subject area which relies on children's ability to be able to recognise and use numbers as well as understand and use mathematical terms when exploring various activities. Their early years mathematical experiences are a starting point for learning how to apply facts, predict and, later on, how to interpret results. Children will also need to be able to look at patterns and describe features of real and mathematical objects using mathematical vocabulary. Do not underestimate the power of language in maths; make sure children understand what you mean when you are working on mathematical ideas, and verbalise things in different ways.

> **Tip**
>
> There is a booklet available online (see Further reading and resources) which highlights the mathematical vocabulary needed from Reception to Year 6. This is a useful toolr as it identifies the words and phrases which children need to be able to make good progress in mathematics.

Numbers – ELG: *'Children count reliably with numbers from one to twenty, place them in order and say which number is one more or one less than a given number. Using quantities and objects, they add and subtract two single-digit numbers and count on or back to find the answer. They solve problems, including doubling, halving and sharing.'*

The early learning goal for numbers relies on children being very secure in their knowledge and use of numbers from one to twenty. You will need to use as many opportunities as you can for counting and using numbers in play and exploration so that they become used to using them. Children need to hear and see the language of maths in their surroundings, so that they develop an understanding of more, less and how many. Use counting songs and rhymes, make comparisons and order numbers, and use them as part of your daily routines. ('How many children are here today? What is the date? How old is Jamie today? How old was he on his last birthday? How old will he be on his next birthday?') You should also have plenty of numbers on display in the learning environment, and children should know where they are to refer to them.

Tip

Use questioning to extend children's learning. Make sure you use open questions so that children have opportunities to describe what they are doing and why. For example, 'Can you tell me how we could share these counters? What could you do first?'

Shape, space and measures – ELG: *'Children use everyday language to talk about size, weight, capacity, position, distance, time and money to compare quantities and objects and to solve problems. They recognise, create and describe patterns. They explore characteristics of everyday objects and shapes and use mathematical language to describe them.'*

Much of this aspect of learning is about investigation and description, so again children will need to have the language to do this. They should also have access to a wide range of resources and materials so that they can explore and talk about features and quantities of different measures. Measures should also be used in context so that children can see the relevance of what they are doing. ('We need to take these bricks to the other Reception class. How can we make sure the bags are not too heavy?') Problem-solving activities, both independent and with others, should give children the opportunity to talk through their reasons for working through an activity in a particular way and describe what they have done.

Tip

Before starting to do a task with children using resources that they have not seen before, allow them some time to play with them and explore them first. In this way, they will not be distracted from what you are asking them to do.

Understanding the world

This is a wide aspect of learning and development and relates to the child and their place in the world. It is part of the curriculum which can really inspire young children as they discover and explore new things; the way in which adults present and talk about places and living things can really enthuse children. They will start by learning about themselves and where they fit into their own family and community, and that their customs and traditions may be different from those of other children. They will also discuss the use of technology at home and in the wider environment.

People and communities – ELG: *'Children talk about past and present events in their own lives and in the lives of family members. They know that other children don't always enjoy the same things, and are sensitive to this. They know about similarities and differences between themselves and others, and among families, communities and traditions.'*

This aspect is about the way in which children develop awareness of events in their own lives and in the lives of others. They may discuss celebrations in different cultures and languages, or invite grandparents in to talk about their own experiences of growing up. Stories and non-fiction books are also helpful ways of introducing different cultures. Make sure your setting has plenty of resources and materials from other cultures, such as clothes or toys, and that children have opportunities to explore other aspects of a culture; for example, cooking through making Diwali sweets.

The world – ELG: *'Children know about similarities and differences in relation to places, objects, materials and living things. They talk about the features of their own immediate environment and how environments might vary from one another. They make observations of animals and plants and explain why some things occur, and talk about changes.'*

This relates to the way in which children explore their own environment and look at others. The outside area is a wonderful starting point for this, as they are able to explore plants, insects and animals, and look at the difference in the environment during and after changes in the weather. You can encourage them to look closely at the features of different plants and animals as well as to do gardening, looking at what happens as plants grow. You should also organise some local walks to shops, libraries, playgrounds or other local community areas, so that children can talk about the features that they notice.

Technology – ELG: *'Children recognise that a range of technology is used in places such as homes and schools. They select and use technology for particular purposes.'*

When working on technology with children, it is important not to think of it in isolation, or as being something which is only to do with computers or tablets. Children should have access to computers in the learning environment, but the word 'computer' does not itself feature in the early learning goal. It is important that you use different kinds of technology and discuss with children the various ways in which it is used. In the classroom environment there should be plenty of other forms of technology which should include wind-up, remote-controlled and programmable toys, interactive whiteboards, digital cameras, and so on. If things break down or stop working (as they inevitably will!) a good problem-solving exercise is to talk about why this might be the case and what the next step should be. Children should also think about uses of technology at home and in a wider context; for example on a walking trip to a local supermarket, you could ask children to look for the different uses of technology which they find (pelican crossings, automatic doors, self-scanning tills, digital scales).

Expressive arts and design

Exploring and using media and materials – ELG: *'Children sing songs, make music and dance, and experiment with ways of changing them. They safely use and explore a variety of materials, tools and techniques, experimenting with colour, design, texture, form and function.'*

Young children need to have access to a range of different media and materials so that they can explore and be creative. This does not only mean painting and gluing, but can also include any sensory materials, or equipment which they can use in their play. Provide larger-scale equipment such as boxes, blankets and guttering, or old saucepans in the outdoor area for children to explore and use. Music and dance should also feature, and there should be plenty of opportunities for children to explore and use instruments and find other ways of responding to different types of music.

Being imaginative – ELG: *'Children use what they have learnt about media and materials in original ways, thinking about uses and purposes. They represent their own ideas, thoughts and feelings through design and technology, art, music, dance, role-play and stories.'*

This area of learning involves children having the opportunity to use materials and equipment in different ways. For example, they should be able to use items either outdoors or indoors, or use small-world play with play dough. Props will need to be interesting and changed regularly, so that children have a rich base of resources to stimulate their imaginations. Adults may need to support children in developing activities, but this should be balanced with those which are child-led. When changing role-play areas with children, it is often helpful for adults to work with children initially and take roles in order to develop their understanding of different situations.

As you become more experienced and confident, you will expand your repertoire of ideas and resources, which should always be changing and evolving. There are many ideas on the internet, for example through groups such as Pinterest, so that you can keep them accessible. You should not think of every aspect in isolation, as children's learning and development will evolve through different activities.

Children who speak English as an additional language (EAL)

Children who speak English as an additional language must be supported effectively during this time, so that they are able to fully access all areas of learning and development. This is because language development is a route to learning and allows us to organise our thoughts and feelings. They may already speak English well or may be just starting to learn it when they come into the setting. Key workers in particular will need to support them and their families where possible in ensuring that they settle in, and encourage their communication in English. In some cases, bilingual teaching assistants will support these children and liaise with parents.

In practice

Does your setting have a policy for children who speak English as an additional language? Although these children do not have special educational needs, they are sometimes given support through the SENCo or inclusion manager. Is this the case in your school?

Parents should understand the importance of completing forms from the setting which ask for information about other languages spoken at home, so that staff are aware and can support them fully. This is key, and parents sometimes do not realise the importance of telling staff about it. Similarly, all staff need to be aware of children who speak more than one language, as it may not always be apparent, and support strategies should be discussed and incorporated into planning. It is also important to remember that speakers of other languages are just as able as other children, and should be challenged as such.

The *EYFS Statutory Framework* states that your school or nursery must support speakers of other languages in two ways:

- Providing opportunities for children to develop and use their home language.
- Ensuring that children have opportunities to learn and reach a good standard in the English language.

Providing opportunities for children to develop and use their home language

When children are learning more than one language, their language development overall may be slightly slower than that of other children, but this should eventually even out. However, development of the home language is very important and influences this, because their home language skills will have a direct impact on how they go on to learn other languages. This is because in order for language learning to take place, children need to 'tune in' to the person speaking and associate a particular language and its vocabulary and sounds with that person. Problems may arise if parents speak more than one language at home, as languages may become confused, so early years workers will need to ensure that they support the development of the home language through working with parents. If children do not appear to be making progress in English, it is important to explore their skills in the home language in case there is language delay. If there are no members of staff who speak the child's home language, you may need to access bilingual support so that you can do this. Children in the nursery or school who speak the same language should be encouraged to play together from time to time, in order to develop these skills.

Ensuring that children have opportunities to reach a good standard in English

For assessment purposes, the *EYFS Statutory Framework* requires that children's communication, language and literacy skills are assessed in English. For their ongoing development and ability to access the curriculum, it is important that these children are given additional opportunities to work with English speakers so that they are able to hear and use the language spoken in context. Many of the play opportunities in the EYFS are perfect for this, for example playing games with others, using role-play and using songs and rhymes. You may need to double-check EAL children's understanding, particularly in large groups and whole-class situations, so that they can develop their speaking and listening skills. You can do this in several ways:

Using purposeful listening – This simply means taking time to give children your full attention when speaking and listening with them – making eye contact and giving thinking time, and checking their understanding where necessary. This can be as part of your day-to-day practice, or it could be a small-group activity.

Providing opportunities to talk – With bilingual children, make sure you provide as many opportunities as possible for them to talk to others and discuss their ideas. If they are more anxious or reticent, they may need support in doing this, or they may need a talk partner or other means of putting their ideas across.

Making sure that you go through any specific vocabulary – If children come into the setting with very little English, you may need to go through any specific vocabulary that comes up as part of a topic; for example, to ensure that they understand it. In addition, you may find as you get to know them that they have particular gaps in their language, for example mathematical or technical vocabulary, and you will need to work on this with them. Use visual props where you can to support language development.

Modelling the correct language – It is important that you do not correct children too much: it is better to repeat the correct language back to them so that they can hear it. Children may become anxious and less likely to speak if they are told that what they are saying is wrong.

For more help and advice when working with children who speak English as an additional language, there are many publications and websites available (see Further reading and resources). Also remember to ask for advice from your SENCo. Although these children do not have special educational needs, your SENCo may have access to support or additional resources.

Chapter 6
Planning, evaluation, observation and assessment

This chapter will look at planning and evaluation alongside observation and assessment, as they often go hand in hand as part of the teaching and learning cycle. This in turn should support your work with children, as you will need to show how their individual learning needs are being met, and how you plan for next steps based on what they know.

If you are new to the role of an EYFS practitioner, there are a number of different things you will need to take into consideration when planning for children. Whatever your role, you should have some input into planning, but due to the nature of the EYFS there should be opportunities for you to put your thoughts and ideas forward, particularly with regard to your key children, as you will know them best. This will help you evaluate learning activities and think about next steps for learning.

All those who work to support children's learning and development are expected to observe and assess how children progress. Observations should take place throughout the EYFS, and assessments at specific times. There are also a number of different types of assessment, both formative and summative (for an explanation of this see page 76). At the time of writing in 2016, baseline assessment is about to be reintroduced to Reception classes so that schools will have a clear starting point from which to measure children's progress. While some may still use the *Early years foundation stage profile* (see www.gov.uk), it is unlikely that teachers will choose to do this, as it will not be statutory.

The main formal assessment in the EYFS is the baseline assessment (see www.gov.uk) when children come into Reception classes, so that schools have a clear starting point from which to measure children's progress.

Planning

The thought of starting your planning can often seem huge and give you a sinking feeling, but this need not be the case. You should not need to spend a huge amount of time drawing up detailed plans – very often they may be changed or amended as the day or week goes on, and you may well find that some of the best plans are written when you are not spending a long time poring over them. Depending on the size of your school or nursery, there will be others around to help you, and previous plans to work from and amend. If you truly are starting from scratch, there are many excellent internet resources, including planning formats, available to help you get started, as well as ideas for topics. While you may have to pay for some of these, many, such as those below, are free and are shared by like-minded people. A few of them are listed here, but this list is by no means exhaustive!

Suggestions for early years planning resources can be found in the Further reading and resources section at the back of this book. It may be helpful to bookmark them so that you can find them easily; you can, of course, add your own ideas to many of them too, and help others.

Long- and medium-term planning

When setting out your ideas for the year, term or topic, you will need to have a clear overall picture of topics which will encompass all areas of learning and development. You should check against the statutory guidance to make sure that children will have the opportunity to experience a wide range of learning activities, while also giving yourself the chance to be flexible and work to children's interests. Long- and medium-term plans should really be a general overview and give you a framework as a learning base. You should not spend too long setting them out, as they may well change as the year or term progresses.

In practice

Find out when the topics or long-term plans in your school were last reviewed. Are all areas of learning covered, or there any changes you can make?

Short-term planning

Short-term plans cover weekly and daily planning, and may sometimes be done for a specific adult-focused activity, when this needs to be broken down. You will probably spend most of your planning time on short-term plans, so that you can be flexible and plan for individual children. Most settings will choose either a detailed weekly or daily plan; it is unlikely that you will do detailed plans for both.

A weekly plan should include:

- a general timetable showing timings (this may be a template)
- adult-focused activities for the week
- continuous provision.

A daily plan may also be used so that you can give more detail about what is happening at different times of the day. An advantage of this is that, inevitably, weekly plans will need to be changed and amended as the week goes on, whereas a daily one may not. However, this will depend on individuals and settings, and staff will decide what is easier for everyone. Whichever way you plan, it is important to make sure that all in the setting, including students and volunteers, have sight of plans beforehand so that they know exactly what is happening and what they are expected to do; it is very difficult to be 'thrown in at the deep end' without having any thinking time. Ideally, everyone will be involved in planning, and there will be opportunities for all staff to be part of the process.

In many settings, long-term, topic and weekly plans are displayed on the wall so that everyone can see them. Nurseries and Reception classes in schools may have a similar planning format, although the kinds of activities will clearly need to be age appropriate for the children. However you choose to plan, make sure that there is space for evaluation and review, so that you have time to look at it afterwards with others and assess what you have done. (For more on assessment, see the final section of this chapter.)

Activity planning

The most important thing to remember when planning is that for a lesson or activity to be outstanding, the learning objective must state what the children will learn, so that you can assess their learning. Make sure you are absolutely clear about what you want the children to **learn**. This is the starting point for any learning activity, whether the children are 3 or 16. In other words, it is important that you do not base it on a description of the activity, but on what you want children to be able to do at the end of it.

Be *very* careful when setting out your objectives, and make sure that they are clear and precise. For example, if you state the objective 'for children to use and understand language relating to weight' as a learning objective, you can see that it is very broad. It is unlikely that very young children will be able to use and understand all weight-related language by the end of the activity. It may be better to say 'to use the vocabulary of "heavier" and "lighter" to describe different objects'. The early learning goals should help you to think about objectives which are realistic and manageable by making you focus on what children need to learn.

The way in which you deliver the lesson and differentiate learning, as well as your use of resources, will also influence final learning outcomes when planning whole-class or group activities. The headings below are to make you **think about** what you need to include in your particular plan, and may be helpful if you are being observed in a school setting.

Prior learning and key vocabulary – This may be useful to note down if you are working on a new area or one which children have not spent time on with you: for example, a topic or maths theme. Make sure you list key vocabulary in this case, and display it later, so that staff and children are reminded to use it throughout the topic and beyond.

Delivery – The way in which you deliver the activity is also very important. Young children will not be able to sit and listen to you talking for long periods of time, and you should not expect them to. They need to play and explore for themselves, as it is part of the process of learning. Make sure that they are involved as much as possible from the start, and if you are working with practical resources, particularly if children have not used them before, give them a chance to explore and use them first. The more practical, the better!

Differentiation – When planning your activity, you will need to think in advance about how you will differentiate the activity for the differing needs of children. You may decide to group them by ability so that you can give more specific focus where it is needed, for example when working on a particular maths concept. In other cases, differentiation will be by outcome and based on how children approach the task. As you become more experienced, you will also be able to see which tasks work better with children of mixed ability, and which should be approached with children who should be grouped together.

Children with SEND (special educational needs and disabilities) and those who are gifted and talented, as well as EAL children – You should include the needs of children with SEND in your planning, as well as those who are gifted and talented, or those who speak English as an additional language. This extra planning does not need to be extensive, particularly if these children have an EHC, as that will set out specific outcomes for them to work on. Children who have an EHC should be known to you, and if you are at all unsure, you should speak to your SENCo or inclusion manager; this is because they may need specialist support or resources.

If you suspect that a child in your class has special educational needs, this is likely to be in one of the following areas:

Communication and language – This may be around the way a child processes language, or the way in which they are able to articulate what they want to say. In some cases it may be necessary to refer them to a speech and language therapist. Autistic children may also have problems in processing language, or in taking what you say literally, and you may need to have a visual timetable for them.

Physical or sensory – This may be caused by a disability or illness which affects the child's mobility, and can also be sensory, such as a visual or auditory impairment. Look out for children who do not appear to be engaged during whole-class activities, and make sure you speak to parents about having hearing or vision checked.

Social or emotional – This will be around the way in which the child socialises and relates to others in the class, and also the way in which they behave. There may be a number of reasons for this, and you should always speak to parents in the first instance.

Cognition and learning – Learning needs will be around the child's cognitive development and the rate at which they progress with their learning. This is likely to be particularly noticeable in literacy and in mathematics.

In some cases, children may have needs in all of these areas, and if you have any concerns, you should seek advice from your school's SENCo or inclusion manager, so that you can plan for them effectively.

For more on pupils with special educational needs, please see Chapter 9. For more on pupils who speak English as an additional language, see Chapter 5.

In practice

Do you have regular contact with your SENCo or inclusion manager to discuss children about whom you have concerns? Keep a record of your concerns by writing things down as they happen, so that you have evidence.

When planning for groups, if you have several children who speak English as an additional language, make sure you do not group them together for this reason; it does not have any bearing on their ability.

Children who are gifted and talented should have learning activities extended for them so that they are able to continue to develop beyond the learning objective, if necessary. Ask more searching questions and see whether they can develop ideas on their own or find their own method of working. Problem-solving activities are particularly effective and will develop thinking skills.

Resources – You should include basic resources on your plan, or those which you may forget, as well as links to any websites that you need, as it is easy to forget these things when you are busy and in the middle of your day. You may need to go out or find specialist resources which are not in your school or nursery, particularly if they are perishable or specific to your topic. Also remember when planning that additional staff, volunteers or students are your most valuable resource. You must set out how you will use them for the activity and be very clear about their role.

Key questions to include – It is sometimes helpful to include key questions on an activity plan, so that you focus on what you want to ask the children in order to develop their learning. You should, however, put these in a prominent place on your plan, or highlight them so that you remember to ask! As you gain in confidence, you may become less reliant on having things written down, and find the right questions easier to ask.

Timings – It may be helpful to think about these when planning – not to be a slave to them, but to give you a rough idea. You may plan for a focused activity to take ten minutes and it may only take three! As you become more experienced, you will learn to 'read' children and to know when their attention is waning, or if the activity does not engage them. In this situation it is better to stop the activity, and to amend or change it next time.

Remember, you do **not** need to use all of these headings or include this amount of detail on every activity, every day: this would not be manageable. Rather, these are helpful to think about if you are going to work on a focused activity with children.

Evaluation

Evaluating learning activities

Shortly after you have completed your activity, daily or weekly plan, it will help you to evaluate what you have done, so that you can think about how it went. You can choose to include as much detail as you wish, depending on what is useful. For example, when reviewing a group activity, you may choose to note down how you could do it differently next time, particularly if you are going to do it the next day with another group. Evaluation is something we are constantly looking at, as it helps us to fine-tune our planning and think about future activities.

Evaluating continuous provision

Evaluation is also helpful when looking at continuous provision; this is because it can sometimes be neglected, as we are doing so many other things! Areas such as sand, water, the writing area, maths area, and so on, should be looked at with a critical eye from time to time. You should think about:

Resources – Do these need to be tidied/organised? Could they be displayed or labelled differently? Do they represent different cultures? Do you need to throw away or replace anything which is broken or damaged? Could resources be refreshed?

The purpose of each area – e.g. To develop language skills, social skills, independence, fine motor skills, to engage curiosity. Are they used in this way? Have the children found additional uses for them?

How children use the different areas – Do the children use everything that is available to them, or are some things more popular than others? (Can you observe them or ask volunteers to do this to check how much and how they are used?) Do you change what is available regularly to keep it 'fresh' for the children and enthuse them? Do you ever ask the children what they would like to see in different areas?

The learning environment as a whole (both the indoor and outdoor areas, as well as different spaces within them) – How do you ensure all children have equal access to learning opportunities? Is the outdoor area always accessible? Who is responsible for keeping it tidy and refreshed? What are the most popular areas/which areas are not used? Are children able to self-serve and put things away easily?

How regularly are structured activities available in each area? – You should try and have a balance of structured activities; that is, activities in which children are working with an adult and which have a specific learning outcome. There should be a good balance between continuous provision and structured teaching.

It may help you to devise a pro forma which could be used to look at current use and plans for development in each area – in this way you will have a clear record and a reference for later planning.

Evaluating other areas

You should also look at daily routines, mealtimes, policies and other practices in your setting from time to time as a staff, particularly if they have been in place for a long time. It will help you to look at them with a fresh eye, so you don't just say 'this is what we do here', as requirements change and ideas can become out of date. It may help to have a rolling programme in place for staff meetings, so that you can do this as part of your practice.

Observation

As you will know, the EYFS curriculum requires you to observe what children are doing, consider next steps and record your observations. Settings will do this in different ways – while some use sticky notes, for example, others may record using a tablet or camera. There are also different computer programs available which support the EYFS profile and will collate data for you. A mixture of photos and notes taken is best, as neither is likely to give enough detail on its own. Schools tend to call each child's profile their 'learning journey' and file observations together under different areas of development, as well as their characteristics of effective learning. Parents can also then contribute to these, adding things which children have done at home for children to share in school. (For ideas on how to encourage parents to do this, see Chapter 2.)

There are a few things to remember when recording observations:

Keep them short – You may only have a few moments to record something a child has said or done, and sometimes you may just need to jot down the minimum and come back to it later. It is important that observations do not take away from the adult's time interacting with children.

Keep them clear and relevant – When carrying out observations, remember only to record things which are significant. By this, I mean that as a staff you can become caught up in having hundreds of observations on each child, which may not be needed. You will know the child and be aware of their skills and abilities, and if you already know and have recorded a number of times that a child is able to recite their numbers to ten, you need not do this again. It is better to look out for new developments or comments from the child which you were not expecting. Observations are particularly useful when:

- children are new to the class and you are starting to build a clear picture of their needs and interests
- children are not making the kind of progress you might expect
- children are showing a particular interest in an activity or idea
- you are monitoring a child for a specific reason.

Keep them clear and dated – What you have written may be clear to you, but make sure it is clear to others, too. It is helpful to initial and put the date on your observations, so that others can discuss the observation with you, if necessary.

Capture quality evidence – Ensure that you focus on the learning process, as well as the end product. Try to capture the child's voice if you can, and reference the context of the learning, if necessary. Use a range of evidence from different people (teachers, teaching assistants, parents) and a range of types of evidence – photographs, learning journals and observations from home.

Remember to observe and record the characteristics of effective learning – When you can, consider how the child is learning (playing and exploring/active learning/creating and thinking critically) so that you have observations on this too.

Remember to include next steps for learning – This can sometimes be neglected, but it need not be long or detailed. Try to focus on what the child needs to do next; for example, if they are having trouble using scissors, they will need more activities to develop their fine motor skills.

In addition, you may use observations to evaluate activities or the use of the learning environment, or to look at the ways in which children interact with one another. Remember to look for things which are popular with children and which encourage them to talk and engage with others. Look for activities which particular children are drawn to and how often they go to them – for example, you may have children who always go to construction activities, or those who only want to play outside.

Assessment

As part of the EYFS you will assess children's learning and development in different ways. Before we look at this, there are two main types of assessment that you will need to know about:

Formative assessment

This is the type of assessment which you are working with on a day-to-day basis. It is your ongoing, short-term assessment of the children as you are working with them, and it informs your planning, as you will need to look at next steps for children's learning.

Summative assessment

This is the type of assessment which takes place at the end of a set time, for example at the end of a term or year. It is a summary of what the child has achieved during that period and is used as a way of tracking pupils' progress long term. Summative assessment used to take place in all schools at the end of Reception with the EYFS profile. However, since June 2016 this has not been statutory, and schools may decide not to do it, although it is likely that they will do some kind of assessment to pass on to Year 1 teachers. The main

EYFS assessment is now baseline assessment at the start of the Reception year; the assessments are set up by approved providers and will look at each area of learning.

You may sometimes ask young children to self-assess their learning, although this is usually reserved for older children. It is sometimes called 'peer assessment' or 'assessment for learning', and it helps them to think about what they have learnt at the end of an activity and how they can improve and build on what they know. At this young age, it may just be a 'thumbs up' or 'thumbs down', or even 'thumb in the middle', following a learning activity, but this will help to give you an idea about what they have learnt and understood.

As children move further up the school, they may start to look at others' work against learning objectives. They may later mark work and underline things which are important and which link to the objective, and give ideas to improve. This will help them to think further about their own progress and how they themselves are being assessed.

During the EYFS, the main type of assessment we use is formative assessment, and you will be more likely to use your own ongoing assessments to check children's progress. You might do this in different ways.

Assessment through observing children speaking to and interacting with others

As already mentioned, observations should not entail huge amounts of work or detract from your own interaction with the children. However, you should keep an eye on the children's records and make sure you have some evidence from each area of learning, as well as the way in which they learn.

Assessment through questioning children

Through speaking to children about their learning, you will be able to get a clear picture about their understanding of an idea or concept, and also their ability to articulate what they know through the use of language.

Assessment through the use of whiteboards or 'thumbs up' (during whole-class teaching)

Ask the children to give a thumbs up or draw a smiley face if they think they can meet the objective, and a sad face if they can't. Ask them to hold it up and show you so that you get a quick overview of their learning.

Assessment through the use of cameras and digital recordings

This might be a piece of film or a sound recording, but it may help you to capture what children have said and how they have reacted, so that you can assess their learning. It is also useful as a form of evidence for the child's learning journey and can be stored either using computer programs or memory sticks, which must be kept securely. Remember, for reasons of confidentiality, always to keep records locked in school and never to take them home.

Informal assessment (through watching and learning about the child)

Remember, you can simply watch children and learn about their needs and interests in this way! Your knowledge of your children will be changing and evolving all the time.

Tips for observations and assessments

- Choose a system that works for you and your team.
- Use cameras and recordings where you can.
- Always date and initial any written notes.
- Talk to children as much as you can.
- Remember to involve parents and include home achievements.

Chapter 7
Safeguarding and welfare requirements

The safeguarding and welfare requirements, which form Section 3 of the *Statutory Framework for the Early Years Foundation Stage 2014*, are part of the responsibility of all who work in early years settings. They are legal requirements which you should follow in order to keep children safe and well, so that they can grow in confidence as they develop and enjoy their learning. For those working in schools and school-based nurseries, there are some differences, but the key points are listed below. For more information on Ofsted requirements and what is required under the inspection framework, see the link to the Ofsted guidance document in the Further reading and resources section at the back of the book.

This chapter will look at the ways in which you can ensure that children under your care are kept safe and well by looking in more detail at the different areas.

The safeguarding and welfare requirements are split into different sections, which cover:

- safeguarding children
- staff qualifications and suitable people
- health and safety
- managing behaviour
- maintaining information and records.

Providers will need to have written policies and procedures in place to ensure that these requirements are met and that all staff and parents are aware of them. In the case of a school-based nursery, these may already be covered by an existing early years or school policy, and nurseries do not need to have separate policies.

Safeguarding children

The term 'safeguarding' has been used to describe both child protection and health and safety, but in this context it is about child protection and keeping children safe from abuse. Your setting must have a child protection/safeguarding policy which will outline what staff should do where they suspect abuse or neglect has taken place. Your setting will have a safeguarding officer (often the headteacher in a school) who is the person to whom you should report any concerns. You should not investigate anything yourself or discuss your concerns with other members of staff. Local authorities will also have a Local Safeguarding Children Board (LSCB) which will provide guidance and support when setting up policies and procedures, as these should be in line with local requirements.

Staff should also have regular safeguarding training (every three years) so that they are up to date with safeguarding issues and are alert to signs of abuse.

Abuse is often carried out by adults who have a close relationship with the child and abusers may include parents, siblings or step-families. In this context, abuse may include the following types:

Physical – This is defined as regularly causing physical harm or ill-health to a child through physical violence. Look out for unexplained injuries and refusal to discuss these, fear of undressing, unexplained absences or changes in behaviour, aggression or bullying, running away, or fear of returning home.

Emotional – This may involve adults or older children persistently telling children that they are worthless, unloved or not valued. It may result in inappropriate emotional responses, withdrawal, eating problems, attention-seeking behaviour, fear of new situations, or regular stealing or scrounging.

Sexual – This involves forcing or encouraging a young person to take part in any sexual activity, including looking at or producing pornographic material, whether they are aware of what is happening or not. It may result in inappropriate sexual awareness, talking to other children about sex, persistent infections in the genital regions, bruises or scratches, refusal to be with certain people, withdrawal, anxiety or aggression.

Abuse of trust – This is defined as a member of staff who is in a position of trust having a sexual relationship with a child under the age of 18.

Neglect – This is defined as a long-term failure of parents and/or carers to meet a child's basic needs, resulting in their failure to thrive and be healthy. It may result in consistently poor personal hygiene, inappropriate clothing, constant hunger or tiredness, untreated medical problems or regular illness, low self-esteem, frequent lateness or absences, or poor social relationships.

Other safeguarding issues of which you should be aware include:

Domestic violence – Children living with domestic violence may have suffered more than one type of abuse, particularly if they witness violence on a regular basis, and may suffer from anxiety or low self-esteem.

Female genital mutilation (FGM) – FGM is illegal in the UK; however, it has been known for families to take girls to another country so that this practice may be carried out. Girls are typically between the ages of five and eight. Look out for behaviour changes, or girls being taken on holiday for 'a special occasion'.

Making sure you are protected

You should be aware of safeguarding issues and make sure that you think about how you conduct yourself when you are around children. Take care not to put yourself in situations which may make you vulnerable. It is very difficult to completely avoid physical contact with young children, as they will often need to be comforted, but be wary and ensure that you are around other people.

- Make sure you do not use your own camera/phone for recording pupils at work. Keep a camera which is exclusively for use in the setting.
- If you have to be alone with a child, leave the door open or tell another member of staff where you are.

- Always maintain professional boundaries with parents, and be wary of what you post on social networking sites.

- If you work with a special needs child who needs intimate personal care, make sure you take advice from your SENCo and setting about how you do this.

Staff qualifications and suitable people

This aspect is about the suitability of staff who work with children. This means that:

- all members of staff will need to have an enhanced DBS (Disclosure and Barring Service) check to ensure that they have no criminal convictions which might affect their suitability to work with children, which needs to be updated every three years

- all staff are suitably qualified to fulfil their roles and that this information is recorded

- all staff have an annual appraisal and that staff training and development is supported effectively

- all staff have up-to-date safeguarding training

- each child has a known key person in the setting

- every setting must have at least one person on site who has a current paediatric first-aid certificate; first-aiders should also accompany children off site on trips when these take place

- there are correct staff-to-child ratios for the age of the children (these are outlined on page 22 of the *Statutory Framework for the Early Years Foundation Stage 2014*)

- all staff working with children have 'sufficient understanding and use of English to ensure the well-being of children in their care'

- a notification is made to the DBS if any member of staff has been dismissed because they have harmed or put a child at risk.

Your school or nursery will need to show Ofsted, when required, that it fulfils these requirements. There is likely to be a staff handbook which should outline how the setting manages this, and which should be run through with new staff as part of the induction process. It is important that staff are aware of the requirements of the *EYFS Statutory Framework* so that they know why the setting does things in a particular way.

Health and safety

Health and safety issues are something that you should be aware of for your own safety and that of everyone in the setting. It is also important so that you can support children's development in looking out for hazards in the learning environment, whether this is indoor or outdoor. Make sure that you have read your setting's health and safety policy and that you know the identity of the person who is responsible for health, safety and risk assessment in your school or nursery. They should carry out regular risk assessments of the learning environment and advise staff if there are hazards which need to be addressed. It is helpful if these are recorded, so that staff can be informed if there are particular recurring safety issues.

Health and safety covers a number of different areas:

Health and medicines – Settings have a responsibility to promote the good health of all children in their care, which includes procedures for preventing the spread of infection. If children have highly contagious infections such as ringworm, conjunctivitis, impetigo or others of a similar nature, it is likely that the policy will be to send them straight home. In some cases, where children are diagnosed with notifiable diseases, the setting will need to report this to the local authority so that any outbreak can be monitored in the area. This includes measles, mumps, smallpox and other diseases. (For a full list see the Health and Safety Executive website at www.hse.gov.uk.) In any case, the school's health and safety policy should give an indication of how long children should be at home when they have more common illnesses such as chicken pox.

Your setting will also have a policy for administering medicines. Be careful – parents will often come in with medicine and ask you to give it to their child. Make sure that you have checked with others before doing so, as settings will have different policies for this. In any case, parents will need to give written permission, and there must be a written record of any medicines which have been administered.

Security – All settings are required to be secure, so that children and staff are kept safe. There are likely to be entry phone or other door security systems, as well as gates and secure boundaries around the grounds and outdoor areas. These will need to be checked on a regular basis to ensure that they are still secure. Visitors should be signed in and out and are likely to be provided with badges so that they can be identified by staff – if you see anyone who does not appear to know where they are or be wearing a badge, you should always challenge them by asking if you can help.

Checking materials and equipment regularly – All equipment in the setting should meet recognised standards of safety, and be age appropriate for the children using it. Materials and equipment which are used on a daily basis by children can easily become damaged when they are in constant use. Keep an eye on them and encourage children to do the same, so that any unsafe resources can be removed and repaired where possible.

Undertaking risk assessment for visits – A member of staff will need to both check that any outside provider has safety checks in place and also assess the risks which may arise as part of the visit. This includes the insurance of any vehicles in which children are being transported. You should also consider adult-to-child ratios, including care of any children who have special educational needs or disabilities. In some schools and nurseries, the risk assessment and steps to take if issues occur are documented as part of the preparation for the visit, but this will be at the school's discretion.

First aid and accidents – As well as knowing your setting's paediatric first-aider and the location of first-aid boxes, you will need to be aware of what should happen in case of accidents and emergencies. When these occur you will need to be able to think and act quickly; take any opportunity you are given to attend first-aid courses. In any event, you will need to record what has happened in an accident book and write down the action that has been taken. Parents will also need to be informed as soon as possible.

Safety and suitability of premises, environment and equipment – Although not your responsibility within your setting, you should also have regular fire and emergency drills so that children and staff know what to do in such an emergency. These should take place at different times of day, including lunchtimes, and not just when it is convenient to do so! Records should be kept of these, so that they can be available for inspection. You should also know that all fire safety and other equipment should be checked regularly. Extinguishers, blankets and smoke detectors should all be checked at least once a year to make sure that they are working. They are also likely to be signed and dated with the time of the last check. Fire exits should be accessible at all times: be careful when setting up the learning environment, and make sure they are not blocked in any way.

Managing behaviour

This aspect is about making sure that settings act responsibly when managing children's behaviour. The guidance does not give a requirement for how this should be done, although in most schools and nurseries there will be a behaviour policy so that all staff know what strategies and sanctions may be applied. Staff will need to be consistent when managing behaviour, so that children know the boundaries and can start to understand the need for rules.

The *Statutory Framework for the Early Years Foundation Stage 2014* is very clear about the fact that corporal punishment must not be given, and that settings must ensure that staff are aware that they would be committing an offence if it were used: physical intervention must only be used to avert immediate danger to an individual. In this case, a record should be kept of where and why it was used, and parents must be informed. (For more on managing behaviour, see Chapter 8.)

Maintaining information and records

All settings which work with children must keep detailed information in different areas, while making sure that it is kept confidential and secure. This is important so that children can be kept safe, and so that the setting can be run efficiently. You will need to know about your responsibilities, which are to ensure that:

- there is a regular two-way flow of information with parents or carers
- information is only used for the purpose for which it was gathered
- records are easily accessible and available
- confidential records are held securely

- where appropriate, information is shared with other professionals working with the child
- parents and/or carers are given access to records about their child
- records relating to children are kept for a reasonable period of time after they have left (usually two to three years).

Information about children – Schools and nurseries will need to keep information about each child; this should be gathered before they start at the setting. This should include name, address and date of birth of the child, as well as the names and addresses of every parent or carer with parental responsibility and a note of where the child normally lives. Medical or health information should also be kept, along with emergency contacts. Parents and carers may need to be reminded to keep names, addresses and contact details up to date, as this is very important and can be forgotten as children move through the setting. Schools may do this in different ways, for example by:

- sending out regular reminders through newsletters
- checking at parents' or open evenings
- asking key workers to check each term or half-term.

Information about staff – The school or nursery will need to keep records on members of staff, such as their qualifications and records about their last DBS check, as well as details about training courses and continuing professional development (CPD).

Information about the setting – Every setting is required to hold information about its day-to-day organisation, which includes:

- name, address and phone number of the provider, as well as any other person living in or employed on the premises
- name, address and phone number of anyone who will be in regular, unsupervised contact with children attending the provision
- a daily record/register of the names of children who are being cared for, as well as the hours they attend and the name of their key person
- certificate of registration (which should be displayed).

Information for parents and carers – The following information should be made available to parents and/or carers:

- how the *EYFS Statutory Framework* is being delivered in the setting
- the range and type of activities and experiences which are provided
- daily routines and how parents can share learning at home
- how the setting supports children who have special educational needs and disabilities
- food and drinks which are provided
- details of all of the school's policies and procedures
- staffing, and the name of their child's key person
- a telephone number for parents/carers to contact in an emergency.

These may be provided as part of the induction process, but there should also be regular updates, newsletters or other opportunities for parents to keep up to date with what is happening in the setting and how they can support their child, as well as information available on websites.

Complaints – You will have a written complaints procedure which will need to be followed in case of a complaint from parents or carers. This will mean that complaints will need to be investigated according to the setting requirements and within 28 days. Any complaint should be documented at each stage, including the result. Settings must also provide parents and carers with details of how to contact Ofsted if they believe the *EYFS Statutory Framework* requirements are not being met.

Every setting is required to notify parents and/or carers in the case of an impending Ofsted inspection; settings are also required to inform parents of the outcomes of an Ofsted inspection and provide a copy of the report.

Chapter 8
Managing behaviour

'Children talk about how they and others show feelings, talk about their own and others' behaviour, and its consequences, and know that some behaviour is unacceptable. They work as part of a group or class, and understand and follow the rules. They adjust their behaviour to different situations, and take changes of routine in their stride.'

(Statutory Framework for the Early Years Foundation Stage, 2014)

This early learning goal as part of the prime area of personal, social and emotional development is fairly short, but as anyone who works with young children will know, it can be a challenging one for some to achieve by the end of the Reception year. If we think about it, in order to be able to achieve the goal, children will need to have a good level of language, be able to make the right choices and also understand the consequences of what they do. Early years practitioners will need to be able to work closely together, as well as with parents, so that a clear message is given to children about expectations of behaviour, and so that they are supported in their understanding of why good behaviour is important.

As a newly qualified teacher or member of support staff, you will be looking forward to meeting your first group of children and getting to know them. However, you will need to make sure that you, alongside other staff, have clear expectations for managing behaviour from the start, and children need to know and understand this from the first time you meet them. Remember to start as you mean to go on – managing behaviour is a fine balance between being approachable to children while remaining firm and setting boundaries.

School policies

Your starting point should be your school's policy for behaviour management. There may well be a separate section for early years, particularly if your school has a nursery. However, it is very important that you have a consistent approach to manage behaviour and that all staff are aware of and work with it, in order for it to be effective. Everyone will need to be aware of what sanctions and strategies they can use; your school's behaviour policy should have a section on this, and it should be regularly revisited at staff meetings. The important thing here is to have expectations in place and to have discussed them with children so that you are prepared – this is better than approaching behaviour management in a reactive way when inappropriate behaviour occurs.

The Department for Education (DfE) has issued a guide for setting a school's behaviour policy (*Behaviour and Discipline in Schools* – January 2016). You can look at this through the government's website at www.gov.uk.

Your school's behaviour policy should outline the following areas.

School expectations for behaviour

There is likely to already be a set of general school rules or a school charter for behaviour which has been devised by older children or the school council. It is helpful to use this as a starting point when speaking to children about expectations, but you may need to reword some of the language so that they understand it. Often, schools will use terms such as the need to 'respect others', which will need to be discussed with younger children. It is then often a good idea for you as a group to agree some ground rules for behaviour in your own space. You should do this as soon as possible at the start of the school year, so that expectations are clear and children know what is acceptable. Remember to think about the language that you use, as this is very significant, and you should ask the children about the kinds of things that are important. Of course, as they are very young, they may need a little guidance, but on the whole, young children will understand the idea and are likely to put forward some good suggestions of their own.

Rewards and sanctions

Schools should make clear both the kinds of rewards and the kinds of sanctions or consequences which teaching staff are able to use in order to manage behaviour. This will develop consistency and ensure that children throughout the school know what is expected of them, and what will happen if they choose to ignore the rules. The early years behaviour policy may be separate from or part of this whole-school model, and should tie in with it.

Rewards are more important than sanctions, as they are a positive way of promoting and maintaining good behaviour. Rewards will vary according to the age and stage of the children – for very young children, they should be used as much as possible in order to encourage positive behaviour and draw attention to it. The kinds of rewards that you might use include:

Verbal praise – This should not be underestimated; as much as you can, praise and encourage children through speaking to them and others about how well they are doing; this will give them a real boost. If you have children who find it difficult to remember what they should be doing, it is very important that you 'catch them being good' and praise them for it, so that they know you have seen them.

Stickers – Many schools use these for good work or behaviour, but make sure yours does before you start to give them out, as some prefer not to and will state this in their policy.

Behaviour charts – These are sometimes used with very young children. Their names are listed on a chart and they are given stickers or a smiley face when they do something good. When they have a certain number by the end of the day or week, they may receive a reward. The chart may be refreshed or started again whenever needed.

Certificates – It is easy to create certificates and print them off to give to children. Many schools have a 'Star of the day' or 'Star of the week' for good behaviour, or will issue certificates on the day if children do something fantastic in order to acknowledge it straight away.

Speaking to parents – Informing parents about good behaviour is another way in which children's good behaviour can be acknowledged and praised. A behaviour book may be helpful if there is limited time to speak to parents, or if the child is being collected by a child-minder.

Talking to another member of staff – If appropriate, telling another member of staff in front of the child about their good behaviour is an effective form of verbal praise.

Whole-class rewards – Marbles or another item are put in a jar each time the class does something good, such as lining up quietly or putting coats on quickly. When the jar is full, the whole class will get a reward.

Sanctions will need to be very clear and, again, very consistent throughout the school and between different members of staff. Before taking action and carrying out any sanctions, make sure you talk it through with the child to make sure they understand – this is often important with very young children, who may not be sure why what they have done is wrong. This is particularly true if you have children who speak English as an additional language, or who do not have a good level of understanding, for whatever reason.

Time out – Separate the child from the situation, or from others if there is a disagreement with another child. This should be for a set period of time, which should depend on the age of the child – for example, with a three-year-old, no more than 3–5 minutes.

Send to another member of staff – If there is a more senior member of staff available, they might speak to the child about what has happened and how the child could behave differently.

Smiley faces/traffic lights – There are three large faces/coloured lights on the wall – one happy, then one with a straight line for a mouth, and finally a sad face (or green, amber and red lights). All the children's names start the day stuck to the smiley face or green light, but names are moved individually to the second face or the amber light if their behaviour is poor, and again to the sad face if it happens a second time. If they try hard their name will be moved back. At the end of the day, parents and the early years manager will be informed about any children on the sad face or the red light.

Speaking to parents/Providing a behaviour book – Sometimes, if there is a child who struggles to control their behaviour, staff may note this down on a daily basis, rather than speaking to them after school in full view of other parents. You can then give the parents these notes to inform them of their child's behaviour.

Often sanctions are listed on a scale in the behaviour policy, so that the child understands what will happen if they misbehave repeatedly. For example, the first step may be time out away from others, the second may be sending the child to another member of staff, and the third informing parents and the setting manager.

In practice

Have you read your school's behaviour policy? Is everyone in your classroom clear on what sanctions and rewards you can use? Do the children know what will happen if they make bad choices?

The role of the adult when managing behaviour

What is your role when managing behaviour on a day-to-day basis? There are several things that you should consider, as positive behaviour management is so important, and you cannot leave it to chance. Remember that children will also watch the way in which you behave.

Think about modelling positive behaviour and the impact of adult behaviour

Children, particularly very young ones, will take their cues from adults, so you will need to think about your own behaviour when you are spending time with them. This might sound obvious, but it can be easy to forget in the course of a busy day. Examples might include:

Showing positive interactions in your conversations with everyone – You should always show that you are interested in others and greet them in a positive way, however busy you are. Develop good relationships with both adults and children, so that children, in particular, trust you – in this way they are likely to respond better to you, as they will feel valued and respected.

Making sure you take the time to actively listen – This is very important, particularly with young children who are learning how to behave and interact with others. Make sure that you focus on what others are saying, look at them and respond appropriately, rather than 'half' listen to them while doing something else.

Showing that you are behaving as you expect children to behave – An example of this might be an adult talking in a loud voice when walking through the school when you are expecting children to be quiet. Children will always notice the behaviour of adults and will be quick to point out if you are telling them to do something that you don't do yourself! It is also important to remain calm when managing behaviour – if you raise your voice and get excited, children are more likely to do the same.

Remembering good manners – This sounds trite, but it is so important, and good manners make a huge difference. Young children want to be like adults and will observe and copy your behaviour. If you are polite and kind to others and treat them with respect it, will follow that children will want to do the same.

Noticing when children are trying hard – If you are aware that a child is trying hard and working on their behaviour, it is important to acknowledge this. Make sure you praise and encourage them for choosing to do the right thing; this will link to the development of their self-esteem and will give them a positive self-image.

In practice

Think about those children who find it difficult to sit and listen or behave appropriately. How often do you 'catch them being good' and praise them for this?

Communicate instructions clearly

This is particularly important for very young children, as they may find directions confusing. Sometimes, as adults, we forget this and give children several instructions at once, for example, 'Pick up your lunchbox, put on your coat and line up for lunch.' This is a lot for a child to remember! You will need to be careful how you talk to young children and ensure that the language you use is age appropriate.

Remember the importance of using positive language

This is often neglected, but it is an important aspect of behaviour management. The type of language you use can make a big difference to children's responses. It is important that you make the *behaviour* unacceptable, rather than the child – for example, if you say, 'Sam, you are a very unkind boy to hurt Eddie like that', Sam might identify himself as an unkind person as his name is being directly linked to his poor behaviour. This is particularly likely if Sam is being spoken to on a regular basis about his behaviour. In this case, if you say, 'Sam, that was an unkind thing to do. Remember our rule for being kind to others', Sam will be less likely to repeat his poor behaviour. You can then follow it up by saying, 'I'm surprised that such a caring boy would do something so unkind, Sam.' This will help you to share an expectation that he won't behave in this way again.

Remember, also, to use the language of choice, and emphasise to children that they are in control of and responsible for their behaviour. For example, you can say to a child, 'Jess, remember our rule about using other people's things. If you choose to take Sonia's things, I will have to put your name on the sad face.' In this way, you are making it clear to Jess that she has chosen to do something wrong, and you are also making it clear to her what will happen if her poor behaviour continues. By giving her responsibility, you will also be helping Jess to be more confident as she understands the consequences of her choices.

Using the correct language is a positive step forward, as it puts the onus on the child in a way that encourages them to think about what they are doing. Its emphasis on choice builds self-esteem and helps children understand that mistakes are a normal part of learning, which give us the opportunity to make a better choice next time.

Think about expectations and making them clear

Much of our work with children when managing behaviour is around talking about our expectations and why these are important. You will need to remind children regularly about what nursery or school expectations are, so that they are aware of this, and it is another reason for consistency among staff. Expectations should always be positive – think about the following:

How to treat others – Young children will need lots of reminding and support to think about how they should treat others and, in particular, how their actions might make others feel. This is particularly important where they have put their own wishes or needs first, as young children are likely to do. You may need to take children aside to discuss things that happen, and it is important to do this as soon as possible after they occur.

How to treat things property – Thinking about resources and items that belong to others might be a new concept for children if the nursery is the first time that they have had an extended time away from home. They are likely to need adults to talk to them about the importance of ensuring that resources are kept safe and tidy for others to use.

How to behave in a shared environment – Being away from the home environment may be very different for some children, particularly if they do not have brothers or sisters. They may find that the rules and expectations are very different, and they may find it difficult to share with others. You will need to make it clear through the way in which you manage behaviour what is and what is not acceptable. You may also find that some parental expectations are different from those of the school, and children might act at home in a way that is not permitted in school. If a child says, 'My mum says I can do/say that', a way round this is to say to children, 'It's one of our rules that we can't do/say that in school.' In this way you will not undermine their parental authority.

Factors affecting children's behaviour

It is important to remember that many things may affect young children's behaviour. Their own circumstances and experiences will clearly have a huge impact on the way in which they behave and how they relate to others. Tiredness, hunger and illness will all have an impact, as will other, more complex issues. You may need to monitor children's behaviour if they start to behave out of character, or in a way that causes you concern. Remember this when reacting to negative behaviour, so that you can ask them about any issues that are upsetting them.

Factors that might affect children's behaviour include:

Changes in their routine – Young children thrive on routine; it is important to them to be clear about expectations and what will happen next. If there are changes in routines, however small, their behaviour can be affected in a negative way.

Home circumstances – Something may have happened at home to cause the child upset. This could be major, such as parental separation, or a new partner being introduced into the home, or something that seems minor to an adult, such as the death of a pet or the loss of a toy. Remember, also, that a change in behaviour can be a sign of abuse, so always monitor closely and note down dates and times (see Chapter 7).

Disagreements with others – Children who have had an argument with a family member or close friend can also feel unsettled and may need to talk about what has happened.

Special educational needs – If a child has special educational needs, this can affect their ability to understand or follow expectations for behaviour. You will need to work with your SENCo so that you understand what is achievable for the child, and frame your responses accordingly.

Speaking English as an additional language – If children speak English as a second or third language, their level of understanding will not be as great as that of their peers. This can cause frustration and emotional outbursts, particularly in very young children, who will find it more difficult to manage emotions. If sanctions are used, make sure children understand why. (See the section on supporting EAL children in Chapter 5.)

Chapter 9
Transition

The term 'transition' is used to describe times of change. In fact, the Foundation Stage is in itself part of a gradual transition to starting school. Times of change may be gradual or sudden, and can take some time to become used to. Typically, if you are working with very young children, there may be a number of different points during their time in nursery or school where you will need to support them through it. This may be individually, in your role as a key worker alongside parents; as part of the settling-in process (see Chapter 2); or as part of the early years team in a more proactive role during specific times of the year when children change classes. Transition may be particularly difficult for children who have a special educational need, such as autism.

Your school should have a transition policy, and you should be familiar with it so that you are clear about what your school does at this time. It is also important that you are aware of the effects of transition on young children and that you are able to work with others to ensure that children are supported effectively. The key points for managing transition are: a) settling in and b) moving year group, although there may also be other periods of transition in children's lives, which we will look at later.

Effects of transition

Young children thrive on routine because it helps them to feel secure and safe and develops their confidence, as they are able to predict what will happen. They will be naturally anxious about change as, being young, they will have had little experience of it in their lives. When they are going through a transition, they can be deeply affected by it and find it difficult, as they may not have the language, understanding or experience to manage it themselves. They will need the help and support of adults around them to feel safe and to ensure that they do not feel unsettled.

Children will take their lead from adults' reactions and the way in which they talk about what is happening, so we need, also, to support parents at this time. If parents appear anxious and make the process seem frightening, children will also be frightened; if adults are overly 'clingy' or tearful about transitions, this will also rub off on children. It is important to make parents aware of this as part of the process, so that they can support their child and make settling-in and transition periods less stressful for them. Similarly, children will need to be given as much information as possible, so that they can be prepared for what is happening.

Settling in

Settling in at the start of school or nursery can be the most stressful transition point and can be overwhelming for very young children, who may experience separation anxiety. This is a natural emotion in young children, as they have built up trust and a feeling of security with parents as their main caregivers. In some cases, children have not spent very much time away from their parents or home, and we should not assume that adjusting to a new environment will be easy or straightforward for them. It is likely that even the most confident children will take a few weeks to feel relaxed and comfortable in their new surroundings. However, if we can make the transition of settling in a positive one, this will also have an impact on future transitions which the children will experience. Children will need to feel relaxed and settled in order to play and learn, so this is an important consideration.

As discussed in Chapter 2, you will need to work closely with parents to ensure that settling in goes smoothly, and you will have to take into account any specific needs which the child has. If the child has special educational needs or a disability, you may also need to work closely with your school's SENCo. The settling-in process may be approached in different ways from setting to setting, and policies may vary. As a newcomer to the school, you may have little control over what the policy is; however, within the environment itself there are things which you can do to support the process and help children to feel less anxious.

Your school's policy may include:

Home visits – Your nursery or school may have a policy which means that staff go to visit the child's home before they start, in order to meet the child and parents. This should really be carried out by the child's key person, as it is a good starting point for the home – school link. In their own home environment, children are more likely to be relaxed and may feel that it is easier to ask questions about the setting. Parents, too, may feel less anxious if they can put a face to a name and ask questions comfortably.

Ensuring you have as much information as possible about the child – Whether this is through forms which are sent to parents, or questions which are asked during the home visit, it is vital that you gather as much information as you can about the child. As well as basic information such as date of birth, place in the family and so on, you will need to be aware of any dietary needs, any issues which the child or family has at that time, any special educational needs or disabilities, and particularly any specific emotional needs.

Visits to the school/nursery – If your school does not carry out home visits, it is likely that children will be encouraged to visit the school or nursery along with their parents at a set time, so that they can look at their new environment and meet their key person. Your setting's policy may include one or several visits – children may stay for a longer period and play, and parents may have opportunities to speak to staff away from their children and meet one another. In many nurseries, parents are encouraged to stay for the first couple of sessions, so that the child feels more relaxed and settled. Parents should always speak to the child before they leave to tell them that they will be back in a little while.

Giving out booklets or leaflets to parents – A booklet containing information and photographs of the setting and normal routines is often available in schools to support the settling-in process. This helps, as it gives basic information and enables parents and children to talk about what they should expect. They should also have access to the school/nursery prospectus, and be able to look through policies which may be on the school's website.

Encouraging children to bring transitional toys or items – These are personal items, such as a cuddly toy, which the child brings in from home in order to help them to settle. They may be allowed by your setting during the settling-in period, so that the child has something familiar with them as a comfort. However, this can sometimes have disadvantages – in some cases, children may become over-reliant on them, and it may be difficult to discourage them later from bringing them in. They may also be very special, and it is important that they are not lost or damaged while they are on site.

Buddy system – Some schools have a buddy system where children in Reception are allocated an older child to look out for them at breaks and during lunchtimes. This helps the younger children and is good for older ones too, as it encourages them to think about the younger children. In some schools, older children will also come into the younger year groups and read with the children on a regular basis.

What **you** can do to help with settling in:

- On the child's first day at nursery, offer to call the parents of your key children to tell them how they are getting on, so that they are reassured.

- Learn children's names as quickly as you can, including correct spellings. Make sure that you are aware of names/surnames of parents and carers too.

- Make sure you keep close to your key children during the first few weeks, and have as much contact as possible with parents.

- Show your key children around the classroom and outside area, and make sure that they know where everything is – toilets, peg, where to find a drink and so on. Remember, also, that they may need to be reminded about this and go over it regularly for the first few weeks.

- Encourage children to complete an 'All about me' book before they start at the setting, with the help of their parents/carers (or older family members), so that you can share it with them and their peers in the nursery or school.

- Remember individual facts about your key children so that you can ask them about things which are personal to them, for example 'How is your new house? Do you have your own bedroom?'

- Read books to children about starting school or nursery; there are many available. These will help children to feel that they are not alone and may encourage them to talk about how they are feeling.

- Encourage any children who are struggling to settle to have a 'buddy' who stays with them and helps them to find their way around. If your school does not have this system, you can allocate them someone in the same class who is more confident and would welcome the responsibility.

- As children start to settle in, give them jobs to do to within the class to make them feel included and to build their self-esteem. This could be, for example, being responsible for a particular area in the room, or an outside area, and ensuring that it is kept tidy, or being in charge of pouring drinks or giving out snacks.

(See also 'Tips for settling in', Chapter 2.)

Moving year group

Clearly, children will need to move year group each year, and although they will get used to it and often enjoy it as they get older, their first time may be quite daunting for them.

Nursery to Reception

Depending on your setting, the children's transition from nursery to Reception may or may not be an issue. This is because in some smaller schools, the classes might run as one Foundation Stage group, and so there will not be a change of staff or classroom, or particular issues with different routines. However, in a larger school, the children are likely to move to a separate space. In this situation, your school will probably have strategies in place to prepare children beforehand, so that the transition is easier for them to cope with. Some possible strategies include:

Visiting the new class to meet staff – This will help children, as by meeting new staff and seeing their new environment they will feel less anxious about what is coming. It is likely to happen on a set day in line with the rest of the school when all classes move up to meet the teacher. The change will probably just be for a short time, so that the children can look at their new environment and talk to the teacher or ask questions about any concerns they might have. Staff may also have a separate meeting with parents around the same time for the same reason. If systems and routines are very different in Reception, the children might benefit from having a booklet to look at alongside parents and carers, so that they get used to talking about the change and what they will be doing in their new environment.

Writing to parents to tell them about the new class – This can be helpful for parents as it will give them an opportunity to talk about the change with their child. You could also hold an information evening so that they can meet teachers. Any information which you can give them about topics, routines, staffing or the structure of the day will help them support their child, and you.

Working with adults – The children could draw a picture or write a sentence about something they like to do for their new teacher. This will enable the children to talk about themselves when they show it to staff.

Encouraging children to talk to adults as much as possible about their new environment – Any kind of discussion is helpful, as it will make children feel less anxious about what is going to happen. Teachers will often enthuse children by telling them the kinds of things that they will do during their time in the class, or talking about things which may be slightly different, now that they are a little bit older.

Giving children responsibilities – As with settling in, responsibilities within the new environment will be helpful in encouraging children to feel more settled and excited about coming to school.

Reception to Year 1

This transition will be a bigger change than nursery to Reception, as children will be coming to the end of their work in the EYFS. In many schools, this is a time of gradual change which starts during the summer term and continues throughout the autumn term of Year 1; this is so that the change is not seen as such a big difference. Ideally, children will start to have fewer child-initiated activities and will be be working towards more 'formal' classroom organisation, which will continue throughout their time in school. They may also start to do more 'whole-school' activities, such as going to assembly or having breaks with older children. These should be gradually increased, so that the children are not overwhelmed and so that they understand what is happening. You will need to work with others to support children in going through the transition, so that they do not view it with too much apprehension.

Other times of transition for young children

As mentioned at the beginning of the chapter, the term 'transition' is used to describe any time of change. Children may also experience a number of changes outside the school or nursery environment, and might need your support. The key when managing these types of transitions is to stay in contact and communicate with parents as much as possible, so that you are aware of what is happening in the home environment and can support their child as much as possible.

If parents have not communicated anything to you but you notice a change in a child's behaviour, the first thing you should do is to speak to them and ask them whether anything unusual or different is happening at home. They may not realise the importance of telling you, or the event itself could have caused them to forget to talk to you about it. The kinds of transition which may occur and which affect children include:

Death in the family – Sadly this may happen while the child is in your class. Although it is most likely to be a grandparent, young children might also experience the death of an even closer relative. The school may need to give some support in this situation, particularly if it is within the child's immediate family. You might need to speak to your school's SENCo in order to give the family other sources of help.

Separation of parents – Even if the home environment has been unhappy for some time, parental separation can affect a child deeply. You may need to work very closely with parents to reassure the child that whatever has happened is not their fault. They will need to have the opportunity to talk about what has happened as much as they need to, so that they can voice how they feel. They may also need reassurance that they will still see the parent who has left the family home and to be told how often this will happen. You will need contact details for both parents so that you can send information to both, and, if possible, invite them both to any school events.

Parent returning to work – Sometimes, when children start at school full time, their main carer may return to work, and this can mean that they are placed in the care of a child-minder or another adult. Although in an ideal world this will happen after they have settled in to school or nursery, this is not always possible, and it may happen at the same time. These children are likely to find settling in quite challenging, as they will be coping with two major changes at once.

Living in a new country – You may have a child (or children) in your class who has come from another country and is starting in school at a time which is different from other children. They may have come from a traumatic situation, speak another language, and find many things very different from what they are used to. Key workers of these children may also need to help their families in other ways through providing information about support groups or giving advice about housing or any entitlements they may have.

New partner or step-parent being introduced – This can be very difficult for young children, especially if the new partner is introduced quickly, or if they do not get along with them, or if it has happened soon after a parental separation. Ideally, it will be a gradual process, so that they are able to develop their own relationship with a new adult at a pace which suits them. Children will be very sensitive to what is happening and are likely to be anxious about changes in their lives – it is important to talk through what is happening when they need to, so that they can come to terms with it. As a child's key worker you will not have control over how the situation is handled at home, but you may be able to talk to parents about what is happening and how they can support their child.

New sibling in the family – Although this is exciting and should be talked about as such, young children may also react to it in negative ways. They may show attention-seeking behaviour, or 'regress' and need help with things which they were able to do before. It can help to give them responsibilities and praise, and to tell them that they will need to help their parents, as there will be so much to do.

Stresses in the family, such as redundancy – Parents may not think that their child has picked up on this kind of issue, but often children will have tuned in to what is happening and be more aware than parents realise; this may then come out in their behaviour.

Moving house/Leaving the school – This can be an exciting time, but children may not always view it as such, particularly if they are relocating and changing school or nursery. They are likely to be anxious about their new environment and missing their friends. If the relocation is further away than the local area, they will need to prepare for it by visiting their new school and finding out about what will happen. It may also help them to talk about how they will keep in touch with their friends in their current class, take photographs and discuss the situation as a group.

Death of a pet – Although this may sound over-dramatic, the death of a pet can affect a young child very much. They may need you to help them by talking about what has happened and discussing ways of coping with it.

These are just a few examples, though of course they are not exhaustive, and any number of things may affect a young child. There may also be other underlying issues for changes in children's behaviour linked to safeguarding and child protection – see Chapter 7 for more on this.

Supporting children who have special educational needs and disabilities

Although transition is difficult for all children, those who have special educational needs and disabilities will need particular support. This can be exacerbated if you and the child's parents are not yet aware of their additional needs. If, through observing them, you think that this might be the case, it will be helpful to record over the settling-in period what you have noticed, so that you can speak to your school's SENCo or inclusion manager and the child's parents, and put some additional strategies in place to support them.

If these needs have already been identified, you should have help from the SENCo or inclusion manager, who will be able to tell you what additional strategies or steps should be put in place to support the child's transition, and to help you to work with parents and any external agencies. Children may come to school with an EHC and might already have access to additional funding, perhaps in the form of extra help from an adult. This is particularly important if staff recruitment or training needs to take place prior to the child's entry into school. The key to a successful transition will be clear sharing of information between the school and the child's parents, as well as any other professionals who have worked with the child, so that all parties have as much information as possible at the start, and there should be a transition meeting in the term before the child enters the setting, so that everyone can discuss their needs and how best to support them.

Children with physical or sensory needs – In the case of physical needs, the child may have specialist equipment, such as a special chair, or a wheelchair or walking frame, to assist them in moving around the room. They may also require toilet adaptations. You will need to check the room's layout to ensure that they have access to all areas. These situations make it even more important for everyone in the class to be aware of health and safety issues, such as leaving chairs sticking out, or not putting items away properly. Children who have sensory needs may also have additional equipment such as hearing aids or loops, or there may be particular resources which help them to access their learning. All staff should be aware of this and be able to help the child, even if the child has a learning support assistant. If children use Makaton or sign language, there will need to be a member of staff trained and available to support them.

Children with social and emotional needs – Children with social and emotional needs may need more support and reassurance than other children, particularly if they are more vulnerable due to their experiences. They are likely to be more anxious and their behaviour may be affected, so you will need to talk with other staff, as well as your SENCo, about how to manage their specific needs.

Children with learning needs – At this stage, children who have additional learning needs may need to be encouraged to join in with some activities, but this should not be over-done. Play activities such as board or other games, and sensory activities such as writing in sand or shaving foam, taking time to talk to them and effective questioning will all be useful ways of supporting their learning.

Children on the autistic spectrum – Children who are on the autistic spectrum will find changes particularly challenging. They have a limited ability to cope with changes in routines and unfamiliar situations, and they may find it more difficult than other children to control their behaviour. Settings will need to work very closely with parents and put steps in place to support the child, preferably before they start at the setting, so that they are able to settle with minimum disruption. The kinds of things which will help will be visual timetables and social stories, which will enable them to predict what is going to happen. Although these will take time to set up, most young children will benefit from them, and you will be able to use them with the whole class.

Children who have speech and language needs – There is a wide range of speech and language needs encompassing different aspects of language, and not all children with speech and language needs will have difficulty with transition. However, it is important that you ensure all children understand what is happening and give them opportunities to talk about and discuss it.

Chapter 10
Continuing professional development

In any profession you will need to engage in continuing professional development (CPD), and careers in education are no exception. CPD has two aspects – it means that you will need to have an annual appraisal or performance management meeting, and you should also undergo regular training, as legislation and curriculum or school requirements change. It is an important aspect of what you do, and should not be seen as something to worry about – rather, it is an opportunity to discuss and build on your experience. This chapter will look at the different aspects of CPD, what to expect from your appraisal, ongoing training, and how to reflect on your own practice.

Main aims of CPD

In addition to keeping you up to date, CPD will enhance your role, as it will make you reflect on your own practice and how you would like to develop.

Being clear about your role
Every role should have a clear job description. Whatever you do in a school or school-based nursery, you should be able to relate it to this. Part of looking at your own development will be reviewing your job description and making sure that it is still a true reflection of what you do in school, as roles will evolve and change over time. You should check that it accurately describes

your responsibilities and duties, so that you are able to support children effectively – make sure you have seen it and read it through.

If you find that your job description is generic, you may be able to go through it with your line manager during the appraisal process and make it more personal to you, adding particular duties which you may perform, such as taking intervention groups or working with specific children.

Your role is also likely to have a person specification, which sets out the kinds of personal qualities which will be desirable and helpful for you to have. These may include:

Be a good communicator – You should be able to interact well with others and be a good listener, as well as being someone who is able to share their thoughts with others in a productive and sensitive way.

Respect confidentiality – As you will be working with young children and their parents, you will be party to sensitive information as you get to know your key children. You will need to be able to share information only on a 'need to know' basis.

Be able to use your initiative – This is important, as during a busy day there may not always be time for you to speak to others about what you are doing. You should be able to use your own initiative when needed, so that you can help others and best support children.

Be a good team player – This means being supportive of others and interested in what they are doing, as well as offering to help and being cheerful about what you do.

Be able to undergo further training – You should be aware that further training will be needed at some point and that you may need to be available at different times of day.

Enjoy working with children – This should go without saying, but you should be able to relate well to children and have fun in the early years environment.

Have a sense of humour – Working with young children can be hard work, and you will need to be able to laugh with others during your day!

How to reflect on your practice

Reflective practice will have been part of your training if you are qualified in your role, and will also be part of your ongoing career development. It means being able to think about what you do and evaluate it by stepping back to look at how it went. For example, you might be asked to work with specific children on a regular basis, but find that you do not have time to discuss what you do with others. You can think about what did not go so well, why the children may have responded in a particular way, or why your approach went as well as it did. You might need to think about the way you have questioned the children, or the way in which you used specific resources. Your school should be able to help you in carrying out reflective practice, and you might find that the process develops your confidence. As you become more experienced, you will start to reflect on your practice as a matter of course, annotating your plans so that you will be able to refer to them if you carry out the same activity at a later date.

The process of reflective practice can also mean looking at other aspects of your role which may be many and varied, and thinking about how you approach each one. For example, if you are also a lunchtime supervisor, you might find that you do not have enough time to prepare for afternoon activities; or your hours may make it difficult for you to have planning time with colleagues. By talking it through with others, it could be easier for you to find a solution to issues which have arisen. It may also be helpful to you to think about other aspects of your role, such as how you handle children's behaviour, or how your position fits into the school overall, and how you support colleagues.

What to expect from an appraisal

Your appraisal will take place each year, and should not be seen as something threatening or to worry about, but as something which is designed to help you to develop professionally. In some schools, teaching assistants and early years assistants do not yet have an appraisal, although this is now rare; most schools now see performance management as an opportunity to support and develop all staff. Many teaching assistants and early years assistants in schools, and all teachers, will now have an official appraisal every year. This is designed to support you, as it will encourage you to reflect on your own professional practice and think about what will help you to develop further in your career. As part of the process, you will need to have some time out to talk about what you find the most satisfying and also the most challenging aspects of your role; you may also want to discuss specific training which interests you, so that you can plan to go on it when it becomes available.

Whether you are a teaching assistant or teacher, your appraisal will run to a similar format, consisting of two or three main parts. It will be carried out by your line manager over one or two sessions, and is also likely to include a short observation of you working with a group of children (more on this later). You should take some time beforehand to think about your role and what you would like to discuss as part of the process. The kinds of questions you might ask yourself include:

- Is my job description a true reflection of what I do?
- What are the best aspects of my job?
- What are the most challenging?
- What training would I like to have?

These will form the basis of your discussion with your manager, and will help you to structure it.

In addition, your line manager will help you to develop a set of personal development targets to focus on over the coming year, so that they can be reviewed at your next appraisal. There should be between three and five of these, and they should be **SMART**:

Specific – The target should be succinct and state exactly what you need to do.

Measurable – You must be able to say how the target can be measured.

Achievable – Make sure that you do not set yourself something that is too difficult to achieve.

Realistic – You should ensure that you have the resources and time to achieve your target.

Time-bound – You should be able to set a time limit to achieve the target.

Your targets should ideally be based on what you are already doing or are planning to do in school. In other words, you should not have to spend a long time thinking about or devising them. In most schools, there will be a whole-school target, or something which the whole staff team are undertaking as part of the school development plan. This is usually a good starting point for your first target. For example, this could be 'To complete training on new iPads for EYFS team' or 'To complete move to the new classrooms'. The second target could be related to something specific to your work with the children and the support you give them, and the third is likely to relate to any areas of responsibility which you have. It is important to keep the targets simple and straightforward and to look at them from time to time to check that you are on track before the next appraisal meeting. Some managers may want to meet up with you halfway through the year to check on progress towards meeting the targets and that they are still achievable.

Induction period for NQTs

As an NQT, you will have an induction period and a school-based mentor or induction tutor to support you through your first year of teaching. Induction is designed to give you a programme of support and development over your first year and also to assess your performance against the core standards which are expected of teachers. Your induction tutor will carry out observations and regular progress reviews, give you feedback on your teaching, and will also be available to support you through your first year. You should see them as a mentor and someone who is there to give advice when needed, as well as a 'critical friend' who can give you constructive guidance. You should also have non-contact time away from your class during your induction year, in addition to your planning, preparation and assessment (PPA) time. NQT non-contact time should be 10 per cent of the total time you spend in the classroom.

For more on the induction process for NQTs, see the government's statutory guidance at www.gov.uk and search for 'Induction for newly qualified teachers'.

Support for teaching and nursery assistants new to EYFS

If you are an experienced teaching assistant who has been moved to the EYFS for the first time from higher up the school, you may find the prospect of working with a new curriculum daunting and consider that you need support. Your school should have an early years manager who is able to help you and work with you as part of this process. You will need to have some kind of additional training, so that you know what to expect from the EYFS and are able to support children effectively in your role. If there is no local training available, your early years manager will need to be able to work with you to go through the statutory requirements and expectations for EYFS staff. You should have access to the *Statutory Framework for the Early Years Foundation Stage 2014*, so that you can look at the legal requirements of the EYFS; you will also need to know how the school plans for the seven areas of learning and development, and how assessment and record keeping are managed. Make sure you seek any support which is available to you, so that you feel able to support the children – you will also need to take some responsibility and read up on your early years policy, as well as keep up to date with best practice in early years. (See Chapter 8 for more on policy in the early years.)

Training courses and keeping up to date

You will have the opportunity to go on training courses as part of your CPD, and will need to keep track of these. They may be related to a subject or area specialism, such as the EYFS, or may simply raise your awareness of new legislation and of topics or ways of working that the school is adopting.

Courses can be run in a variety of ways:

For the whole school – These may be run as part of staff meetings or INSET days on school premises and will be compulsory for all staff to attend, for example in the case of safeguarding, health and safety, or minor first aid. If your school takes on a new initiative or computer assessment program or wants all staff to adopt a particular way of working, this is the quickest way of training everyone.

For specific members of staff – Following your NQT year, as a teacher you are likely to be a subject leader. In this capacity, you will need to go on courses that will help you with managing your particular subject. There are also likely to be regular updates or forums locally, so that you can meet others who are in the same role and discuss any changes or issues that you should know about. Similarly, if you are a school governor or have a responsibility for an area such as drugs awareness or health and safety within the school, you may be asked to go on courses to keep you up to date with what is happening nationally.

For those who have expressed an interest in learning about a particular subject or curriculum development – These may be in the local area or further afield, for example at a conference or other event with guest speakers and workshops. These types of courses are useful as they will help you see the bigger picture, and give you the opportunity to network with others. In some cases you may be asked to feed back to others at the school and pass on to them what you have found out at a staff meeting.

It is very important for your own information that you keep a list of training courses which you have attended. This is because as your career progresses, you will find that you have been on so many that you will not remember when you attended specific training, the detail of what it entailed, or how up to date you are. Your school might keep a list in your professional development file, but you may not remember to take it if you leave, and so it is a good idea to get into the habit of keeping track of what you have done with any notes and certificates at home. You should also keep a copy of your personal development record, so that you can look back over it for your own information. It is also very helpful to have when you are applying for jobs or additional qualifications, as you will be able to see exactly when you had your training and who delivered it.

Being observed

Many people are anxious about being observed by others, but it is part of our ongoing development and is designed to help us to move forward. If you are going to be observed as part of your appraisal, make sure you are fully prepared by planning carefully. You will also need to send your observer a copy of your plan, so that they know what they are coming to see. If something happens on the day and you are unable to proceed with what has been planned for any reason, you should let them know as soon as you can, and reschedule for another time, rather than try to carry on when circumstances have made it difficult to do so. Working with young children is always unpredictable, and your line manager will understand this.

You might also be observed as part of the interview process when you apply for a new job. This will be viewed slightly differently by your observer, as you will not know the children's abilities or be familiar with the classroom. The main thing to remember is to include your objective, and not to try to do too much – be very clear about what you want the children to do. If you plan to use technology, have something up your sleeve in case it goes wrong. Your observer will be looking mainly at how you interact with the children, how you manage behaviour, and whether your manner is professional.

Teaching and nursery assistants – Make sure you speak to the teacher well in advance, as you should be able to select what kind of activity you will be doing with the children for the observation. You are likely to be working with a group, so check things like seating arrangements (plan who will be next to each other). Check things like vocabulary which you may want the children to be familiar with, and look carefully at how you will present the activity. If you are using new resources, make sure you are familiar with them and give the children some time to play with them and explore them before you start the activity, otherwise they will be very distracted.

Teachers – This will be similar to observations you have had on teaching practice and as part of your NQT year. You will need to supply details on your plan, including:

- date and timings
- objectives, or what you want the children to learn
- what has been their previous experience of the subject
- how you have planned for different abilities and how you will assess children's learning
- starter and main activity, and how you will finish the session
- resources, including assistants and volunteers
- key vocabulary and questioning
- any ICT you will be using.

Make sure you are thoroughly prepared, particularly as you will need to have a lot of resources ready and set up. A tip for any lesson which is being observed is to have an unusual starting point – bring something in to show the children or start with something unexpected, in order to grab their attention and that of the observer.

Following your observation you will need to meet with your observer to discuss how the session went. This should be as soon as possible afterwards, while it is fresh in both your minds – not a week or two later. You are likely to be asked what you feel went well and what could have been improved, so have a think about this before your meeting – this is to encourage you to think about your practice on a daily basis.

Qualifications for early years workers

There is a wide range of early years qualifications that may be used to work within a school nursery or Reception class at different levels. You may have previously worked in a nursery or pre-school, or have been a child-minder and decided to change direction and try a school-based environment. In any case, the different levels of qualification are similar to those for teaching assistants: Level 2 is equivalent to a GCSE level and Level 3 is more of an A level-equivalent qualification. As you are already working in a school, you might wish to develop your qualifications and work at a higher level. When looking at qualifications, check that they will be valid for what you want to do and are nationally recognised. At the time of writing, the full list of early years qualifications at different levels is available on the DfE website: http://www.education.gov.uk/eypqd/qualifications.shtml

Qualifications for teaching assistants (TAs)

The teaching assistant's role has changed dramatically over the past 15–20 years. From their origins as a 'mums army' who came into schools to hear readers and help with painting many years ago, the majority of teaching assistants are now qualified professionals who undertake a wide range of roles in primary and secondary schools, and teachers find their work essential to the smooth running of a class. They also carry out vital work with individual children and small groups, and give mentoring and other pastoral support to children and young people.

As a TA, you may or may not have professional qualifications or recognition. There is no legal obligation for you to have them at present, although many schools do advertise jobs which list them as a requirement. Workforce remodelling in 2003 was designed to free teachers from a number of listed tasks, which they were able to ask teaching assistants to do for them. Work-based qualifications at NVQ Levels 2 and 3 were introduced in 2003 as a direct result of this, in order to clarify the different levels at which teaching assistants work and to make it easier for employers to see their level of skills and experience. Teaching assistants were encouraged to undertake national vocational qualifications (NVQs) and higher-level teaching assistant (HTLA) training so that they would be able to show potential employers the standard they had reached in the profession. The number of teaching assistants in schools in England has more than trebled since 2000 to 243,700 in 2015 (*Source: Education Endowment Foundation, 2015*), and they now carry out a wide range of roles in primary and secondary schools. HLTA status is Level 4 equivalent, but is not a qualification; it is designed to show that you are working at a high level as a teaching assistant. In some schools, HLTAs will manage other support staff and, in some cases, will be on the senior leadership team (SLT) and carry out performance management. It is now also possible to do a foundation degree in Learning Support, which is available through colleges and online; this can be a stepping stone to a teaching qualification.

Keeping up to date and looking ahead

You should always keep in mind that roles are ever-changing and that you will need to keep up to date. Read around the subject, be aware of what is happening in the news and check early years websites and publications for what is new. Always attend early years forums in your area if you can, go to conferences or the early years shows, and visit other schools to see different ways of working. Within your own school, you can visit other teachers and classrooms to get ideas and discuss different ways of working. If opportunities come up, always take them if you can, as they will widen your experience and may take you in a different direction. Always keep learning.

Chapter 11
Extra tips for a happy classroom

For a classroom to work successfully, you will need the children, whatever age they are, to feel happy, valued and motivated to work. The routines and organisational systems that you put in place from the start will help both you and the children to feel settled and calm, and will enable everyone to have a sense of belonging in your room and within your team.

During your first few years in the classroom, you will pick up a wide range of tips and ideas which will help you to manage in your new role. You will need to find out what works – and what doesn't – and make a note, so that you are able to plan them in to your schedule. Working in early years is very tiring and can sometimes feel chaotic, but it is also a very rewarding age group. Keep your planning and write things down as you go, so that you remember them – otherwise you may not.

After lots of thought and deliberation – and requests to other professionals working in early years – I have come up with a few action points which might help you as you develop your routines and classroom management skills.

Set the boundaries

From the very first day, you will need to be clear about both setting the boundaries within the room and the expectations which you have of the children. If you are working as a TA or nursery assistant, you will need to have discussed routines and expectations with teaching staff, so that the whole team is clear about how you will address this with the children, and how this will fit in with school policy (see also Chapter 8). Although you will need to get on well with children as part of your role, your intention should not be to 'befriend' them, nor to be so nice to them that they step over the line. It is very important to get this right from the start, as clear boundaries and high expectations will help you to gain their trust and ensure that they respond to you in a positive way. Always be confident in what you are saying to them, and wait for them to be quiet before you speak; if you allow them to talk over you, you are telling them that it is okay to do this. In a similar way, if you are talking to another adult, and a child comes up to you, they should always wait for you to finish what you are saying (unless it is urgent, of course). 'Expectation' is the key word here. If adults have high standards and expectations for behaviour and have discussed these with the children, they are far more likely to respond positively.

Keep to routines

As previously mentioned, routines are very important to young children as they help them to feel secure and develop their confidence. When they start in a new setting, they will need to quickly pick up the routines, so that they know what is going to happen next. Most classes will have a routine which they go through at certain times of day – for example at the start of the day there will be a register and counting who is there, looking at the weather, checking the day of the week and talking about what will happen that day.

In some schools, classes will have a visual timetable which will give a series of illustrations showing what will happen during the day in the correct order. These are often used to help children in special schools, but they are also helpful with very young children who may need reassurance. Children who are anxious may benefit from going through the timetable with an adult at the start of the day, or sometimes, it may be part of the routine that it is done with the whole class. Illustrations for visual timetables may be found on a number of websites (see the end of the chapter for these).

There are also likely to be routines for snack time, story time, tidy-up time, lunchtime and home time, which the children will become used to. The day needs to be broken up into different sections, as this will help young children to stay focused on what is happening.

At the start of the year, children in Reception should not have playtimes and assembly times with older children, as these may be difficult and overwhelming for them. However, during the summer term, these should start to be built in to the routine, so that by Year 1 they are able to mix with other year groups for whole-school or key-stage events.

Give children ownership of the space

A sense of ownership and belonging is important to children. They will need to feel proud of their surroundings and part of them – the whole-school family as well as the classroom environment. One way of doing this is through keeping it tidy and organised and having this as one of your expectations – children will not feel proud of their classroom if adults do not foster ownership of them. Remember to tell them that they are all part of the class, talk to them about how we do things in our class, and put up signs with language such as 'Welcome to our room', or 'Our class rules'. Displays will need to be clear and show the children's names on their work where they are clearly visible. Your room will probably have a 'birthday wall', where children can find their name and birthday, and their names should also be displayed on their pegs and other items which are personal to them, so that they know where to find what they need. (Make sure also that the children are able to recognise their own name!) You may display photos of the children at work in different areas of learning and use these as prompts to talk to them about what they have done.

Promote children's independence

One of the early learning goals for personal, social and emotional develop-ment is that of self-confidence and self-awareness. Children of this age are developing their independence skills and learning how to do things for them-selves. However, they will often ask for help from an adult without trying first – we need to encourage them to 'have a go', so that they can learn by doing. This will start as soon as they come through the door in the morning, when they need to take off their coat and hang it up, or put a book bag away in the right place. There will not be a sufficient number of adults to go round at times when children need to put on their coats, change for PE or give out the fruit, and children must learn to do these kinds of things for themselves.

When a child can't put their coat on, tell them to try the magic coat trick. Lay the coat on the floor, the wrong way up with the 'head' end of the coat at the child's feet. Then ask them to put their arms in and take the coat over their head, pushing their arms down into the sleeves as they go.

Encourage them to help one another: if they are struggling to do up their coat or shoes, for example, get them to ask one of their friends to help before asking an adult. This takes pressure off the adults while encouraging children to do things for one another and themselves.

Encourage a 'have a go' attitude

Some children come to school with very little confidence and do not have much experience of trying out new activities for themselves. They may say 'I can't do it' or be very reluctant to have a go. You might need to encourage them through working alongside them on new activities, or through asking their friends to do this to support them. If this does not work or they do not feel comfortable doing it, don't force them, but try to encourage them again at a later date. It may take some time for them to feel that they want to have a try, because of lack of confidence or fear of failure. Focus on those children who have tried new things and give them praise for having a go, so that it is clear that this is what you would like to see.

Get the children's attention before you speak to them

When the whole group is working on learning activities, at some point you will need to tell them to stop and tidy up. There are a number of ways of doing this, and we all find different ways effective. The main thing to avoid is raising your voice too much, as children sometimes do not hear you, and you may end up calling out louder and louder, which is not sustainable over a long period.

In some classes, teachers will use a tambourine or bell to get the children's attention when they are all busy doing different activities; when the children hear it, they know it is time to stop. Others clap out a rhythm which the children repeat back. If they don't do it the first time, repeat until they do it and are all listening. Or try 'give me five' – the children have to stop and hold up their five fingers spread out, each finger representing what they need to do:

1 eyes looking
2 ears listening

3 hands empty

4 mouth closed

5 body still.

In some classes, teachers have a special thing which they say to get the children's attention before giving them an instruction, such as 'Hands on top: that means stop!' (everyone puts their hands on their head and the adult waits for quiet) or '1, 2, 3: eyes on me!'

Tidying up

As well as the tips above for getting attention, in some classes there may be a song which adults start to sing, or they may put on 'tidy-up music' so that the children know it is time to put things away. When they hear it, they should know what they have to do. Between two and four minutes is usually a good length of time. Children are usually very responsive in this situation, although some will need reminding more than others about what they should be doing.

The website www.classtools.net has a countdown timer and includes some pieces of music already – helpful if you have a whiteboard, as the children can see the numbers counting down. Speaking from experience, calmer music is generally better for this, as the children can get very excited when they are trying to tidy up before the music gets to zero!

Or try a tidy-up song for everyone to sing as they do it. The following is frequently sung to the tune of 'London Bridge is falling down':

Everybody tidy up, tidy up, tidy up; everybody tidy up, it's tidy-up time

Everybody sit down, sit down, sit down; everybody sit down, it's carpet time.

(The children join in; the words are then substituted with any other instruction, such as 'sit down', 'line up', etc.)

Sing your way through the day!

Singing is a very useful tool when working with young children. You can use it to calm them down, get their attention, and as a learning tool to enhance what you are doing, as well as simply for enjoyment. Sometimes, if children are over-excited or just can't settle, singing can really help to bring them all together again. I have found that by learning just three chords on the guitar, I could cover a wide range of songs. You can build songs in to your routine and sing them at key times of day, so that the children join in. If you do not play any kind of instrument or feel confident using music, there are many books available with helpful suggestions, and you can build up your own repertoire of songs with the children. The website www.singup.org has lots of ideas and help, from songs to greet the children in the morning, to Christmas or other seasonal ideas. If you have them all sitting on the carpet, just ask one child to come to the front and tell you their favourite song – they will all want to sing! I have included a few tried and tested ones here:

Rhyme to get children's attention when on the carpet

- Sit very quietly, sit very quietly (whispered)
- Do good sitting, do good sitting (thumbs up action – for 'good' and arms crossed – for sitting)

- Sit very quietly, sit very quietly (whispered)
- Do good listening, do good listening (thumbs up action – for 'good' and cup ear – for listening)

- Sit very quietly, sit very quietly (whispered)
- Do good looking, do good looking (thumbs up action – for 'good' and BSL sign for looking – point to eye and move arm out)

Song for the start of the day

(to the tune of 'Frère Jacques')

Come and sit down, come and sit down

Close your lips, close your lips

Show me your good sitting, show me your good sitting

Well done, well done.

Also to the same tune. . .

Eyes are watching, ears are listening

Lips are closed, hands are still

Feet are very quiet, you should really try it

Listening well, listening well.

Song to learn days of the week

(to the tune of 'The Addams Family')

Days of the week (*clap clap, you're meant to click your fingers really, like the original song, but young children find it easier to clap*)

Days of the week (*clap clap*)

Days of the week, days of the week, days of the week (*clap clap*)

There's Sunday and there's Monday, there's Tuesday and there's Wednesday, there's Thursday and there's Friday, then there's Saturday.

Days of the week (*clap clap*)

Days of the week (*clap clap*)

Days of the week, days of the week, days of the week (*clap clap*).

Song for the end of the day

(to the tune of 'Here we go round the mulberry bush')

Shake a friend's hand and say goodbye, say goodbye, say goodbye,

Shake a friend's hand and say goodbye, we'll see you all tomorrow.

(then ask what day it will be tomorrow and sing the verse again with the day inserted)

Shake a friend's hand and say goodbye, say goodbye, say goodbye,

Shake a friend's hand and say goodbye, we'll see you all on Tuesday.

It's been so nice to play with you, play with you, play with you,

It's been so nice to play with you, we'll see you very soon.

What did you learn today, learn today, learn today,

What did you learn today and with who(m)?

(the idea behind this is that the children will be able to tell their parents
   what they have done as they have just been thinking about it. . .)

**Finally, here are some quotes from teachers and teaching assistants who
have been new to the job or moved from a higher age group; they include
things they wish they had known when they started in EYFS:**

*'Have a simple list of tasks ready for the children in a class who need atten-
tion or may become disruptive. It works a treat when you need to calm them
down, and gives them a real sense of pride.'*   Hannah

*'Ask for phonics training. When I first went into Reception as a TA, I had no
idea and was literally left to do it!'*   Jenny

*'No one tells you how exhausting it is! And how silly, everyday things
delight little ones. I have a little list of tasks and the children love picking
one.'*   Lydia

*'I always find that getting down to their level and joining in their games
makes for a great relationship – then they are more likely to talk to you! So
much can be gauged by just having conversations with them.'*   Sue

*'Always be prepared and expect the unexpected! It helps if you have certain
things to hand, such as a notepad and pen for the unexpected observations.
And don't forget the anti-bac gel!'*   Helen

'I taught in KS1 and KS2 before I became a TA (after being ill), first in Year
5/4/3, then in early years. I wish I had known:

- just how physical the job is
- that I had no knowledge of how teaching is achieved in this year
  group
- that the other adults are so run off their feet, they don't have time to
  tell you what is required

- that they have very little in the way of resources (and that they don't always go in line with LOs) and very little in the way of money to replace them

- that I won't get a chance to have a drink, much less go to the toilet!!

- how lovely the children are, if somewhat challenging!!!

- what a great team we have!!!!'   Carol

'When I first went into Reception just 2 years ago, after having worked in KS2 for the previous 16 years, I had no idea how to 'do observations' on the children, and I didn't know what I was supposed to be looking or listening for!'   Angie

'Don't show shock or surprise; learn to have a poker face. If you laugh, they laugh; if you are upset, they tend to get upset. Enjoy your inner child. Young children enjoy adults joining in. So if you can play in the role-play area, play. . .If there's a space to paint, paint. Put on silly voices when reading a story. Play hopscotch; if you can't hit a ball with a bat, still play and laugh when you miss. . .NEVER, EVER, ever, reveal a fear of creepy crawlies!'   Andrea

'I've worked in early years for the last ten years. I've been a Reception TA since September – my advice to anyone is: don't take yourself too seriously and make sure you have comfortable shoes on (you never know when you might have to run!) If on the door/gate in the morning, greet every child by name and with a smile (no matter how much they drove you to despair the day before). Make sure you like your own name, as you will be hearing it a LOT and, above all, remember they are only little; they are going to be in education for a long time, so make their first year fun!'   Julie

'My first-ever job as a TA started in Reception and I wasn't told what to expect. I was left feeling stupid and having to ask lots of questions. You need training and support to be supportive. Once I got into my stride, I was okay. I built up a fidget bag for the less attentive and a couple of autistic pupils to help them stay on the carpet and join in.'   Sarah

'Be prepared to deal with every kind of bodily fluid – either cleaning it up or wearing it. Don't spend a fortune on clothes and shoes. You spend so much time sitting or kneeling on the floor!'   Carol

'*How much my feet would ache, and my back! Watch others around you to get tips. Wash your hands regularly. Hug children if they need it. Wear flat shoes and trousers. Be prepared to get your hands dirty, and everything else! Use your imagination with ideas on games to play. Read, read, read! Not having enough time to do all the things that will be required of you. Not realising how attached you will get to the little ones you look after. Just having to get on with it even when there aren't enough staff to go around. That you will need to stock up on cold and flu stuff, painkillers, etc! But, above all, how much fun you will have, and if you're not having fun, you're not in the right job!*'   Nicki

Glossary of abbreviations and acronyms

AfL	Assessment for learning
ASD	Autistic spectrum disorder
CPD	Continuing professional development
DBS	Disclosure and Barring Service (Formerly Criminal Records Bureau or CRB)
DfE	Department for Education
EAL/EFL	English as an additional/foreign language
EHC	Education, Health and Care plan
ELG	Early learning goal
EP	Educational psychologist
EYFS	Early Years Foundation Stage
HLTA	Higher-level teaching assistant
HSE	Health and Safety Executive
KS1/KS2	Key Stage 1 (Years 1 and 2) Key Stage 2 (Years 3–6)
LSCB	Local Safeguarding Children Board
NVQ	National Vocational Qualification
NQT	Newly qualified teacher
Ofsted	Office for Standards in Education
OT	Occupational therapist
PPA	Planning, preparation and assessment
SALT/SLT	Speech and language therapist
SEN(D)	Special educational needs (and disabilities)
SEN(D)Co	Special educational needs (and disabilities) co-ordinator
SLT	Senior leadership team

Further reading and resources

This section contains references and suggested books and websites which may be useful for some of the topics covered in the book. There is also space available for you to add some of your own, so that you have them together in one place.

Chapter 1: The role of the adult in the early years

Websites

www.gov.uk – *Statutory Framework for the Early Years Foundation Stage 2014.*

www.foundationyears.org.uk – *Development Matters in the Early Years Foundation Stage* – This document consists of non-statutory guidance materials and is designed to support EYFS practitioners in implementing the statutory requirements of the *EYFS Statutory Framework*. It was originally produced by the charity the British Association for Early Childhood Development.

Chapter 4: Enabling environments

Books

There are some excellent books available to give you ideas and inspiration when setting up your classroom. Try Alistair Bryce-Clegg's book: *Continuous Provision in the Early Years* (Featherstone Education, 2013), or Helen

Bilton's book: *Playing Outside: Activities, ideas and inspiration for the early years* (David Fulton Publishers, 2005).

Websites

www.early-education.org.uk – A good selection of resources available for enabling environments, which are listed under areas of learning.

www.ecersuk.org/11.html – The ECERS website provides a checklist for going through learning environments and looking at provision.

www.twinkl.co.uk – This site provides a number of labels and other free resources which can be printed off; some are more general, while others are topic related.

Chapter 5: Areas of learning and development

Literacy

There are plenty of websites to support you with literacy, particularly phonics:

www.gov.uk – *Letters and Sounds: The Principles and Practice of High Quality Phonics* – This is the Department for Education's official guidance on phonics.

www.letters-and-sounds.com – Resources to support teaching phonics.

www.mrthorne.com – This site goes through the letters and sounds in phase order and video by video to support children's learning. It is also available as an app.

www.phonicsplay.co.uk – Available on subscription, but you may find that your school already subscribes to it.

Mathematics

Mathematics Vocabulary – ref 0313/2000 – This Department for Education National Strategies booklet is very helpful for identifying key mathematical vocabulary for each year group. It is currently in the National Archives, but is available if you search for 'Mathematical vocabulary booklet', or simply insert: 'ref 0313/2000' into a search engine.

English as an additional language (EAL)

100 Ideas for Early Years Practitioners: Supporting EAL Learners by Marianne Sargent (Bloomsbury Publishing, 2016).

www.dfes.gov.uk – Look here for information under 'EAL learners' or 'English as an additional language'.

www.education.gov.uk – *Supporting Children Learning English as an Additional Language: Guidance for Practitioners in the Early Years Foundation Stage.* This document was produced under the National Strategy in 2007, but it is still useful and has some helpful ideas:

http://webarchive.nationalarchives.gov.uk/20130401151715/http://www.education.gov.uk/publications/eOrderingDownload/DCSF-00683-2007.pdf

http://www.naldic.org.uk/eal-teaching-and-learning/outline-guidance/early-years/ – NALDIC (National Association for Language Development in the Curriculum).

Chapter 6: Planning, evaluation, observation and assessment

Websites

www.gov.uk – The *Early years foundation stage profile* can be found here.

https://nrich.maths.org/early-years – Excellent maths and problem-solving resources.

http://www.primaryresources.co.uk/ – Look under the 'Foundation' section.

www.tes.com – The *Times Educational Supplement* has a great range of resources under 'early years planning'.

www.twinkl.co.uk – Great for lesson plans and teaching packs.

Chapter 7: Safeguarding and welfare requirements

www.gov.uk/government/uploads/system/uploads/attachment_data/ file/458588/Early_years_inspection_handbook.pdf – This is the link to the Ofsted guidance and what is required in the early years under the inspection framework.

Chapter 8: Managing behaviour

www.gov.uk – The Department for Education produced the following guidance in January 2016: *Behaviour and discipline in schools: Advice for headteachers and school staff*

Chapter 9: Transition

Books
Sue Allingham: *Transitions in the Early Years: A practical guide to supporting children between early years settings and into Key Stage 1* (Early Childhood Essentials, 2015).

Ros Bayley and Sally Featherstone: *Smooth Transitions: Ensuring Continuity from the Foundation Stage* (Featherstone Education, 2014).

Anne O'Connor: *Understanding Transitions in the Early Years: Supporting change through attachment and resilience* (Routledge, 2012).

Websites
www.childbereavementuk.org/support – This site has some useful information and help with supporting young children dealing with grief.

www.teachfind.com – There are a number of videos on transitions from Teachers TV on this website.

www.youngminds.org.uk – This organisation supports children and young people through different transitions at all stages.

www.youtube.com – Numerous videos on transition.

Chapter 10: Continuing professional development

Websites

www.education.gov.uk – Early years qualifications list.

Educationendowmentfoundation.org.uk – Charity that seeks to improve the educational outcomes of the poorest pupils in the UK. Also provides statistics on the positive impact of high-quality, trained TAs.

www.foundationyears.org.uk – This site has resources and guidance for parents and professionals.

www.gov.uk – Induction for newly qualified teachers (England): statutory guidance for appropriate bodies, headteachers, school staff and governing bodies.

www.napta.org.uk – National Association of Professional Teaching Assistants. This body has been set up to help TAs with their professional development. The site has free resources and FAQs to support training needs.

www.nurseryworld-magazine.co.uk – This magazine has articles on new initiatives, as well as guidance on practice.

www.tes.co.uk – The *Times Educational Supplement* has lesson plans, tips, videos to support your practice, and forums to give you advice.

Chapter 11: Extra tips for a happy classroom

Helpful sites for every day

These sites will be constantly changing and added to, and you should build up a bank of your own and add to them as you go, so that you can use them when you are planning and looking for ideas.

www.classtools.net – The countdown timer for tidy-up time.

www.uk.pinterest.com – You can save your own early years ideas here and steal some from other people!

www.primaryresources.co.uk – Help with lesson planning.

www.singup.org – This site has lots of helpful songs; you can join for a trial period. You may even find that your school already subscribes; check with the music co-ordinator.

www.twinkl.co.uk – Lots of ideas and resources for your room, including those for display and visual timetables.

Index